ANSWERS TO COMMON QUESTIONS ABOUT

Heaven & Eternity

ANSWERS TO COMMON QUESTIONS ABOUT

Heaven & Eternity

Timothy J. Demy
Thomas Ice

Published by Kregel Publications, a division of Kregel, Inc., P.O. Box 2607, Grand Rapids, MI 49501.

Library of Congress Cataloging-in-Publication Data
Demy, Timothy J.
    Answers to common questions about heaven and eternity / Timothy J. Demy and Thomas Ice.
        p. cm.
    Includes bibliographical references.
    1. Heaven—Christianity—Miscellanea. 2. Future life—Christianity—Miscellanea. I. Ice, Thomas. II. Title.
    BT846.3.D46   2010   236'.2—dc22   2010046787

ISBN 978-0-8254-2657-5

Printed in the United States of America

11 12 13 14 15 / 5 4 3 2 1

Contents

Part 6: What Do Other Religions Teach About Heaven and Eternity? 83

Part 7: What Is the Significance of Heaven for Today? 96

About This Series

The Answers to Common Questions series is designed to provide readers a brief summary and overview of individual topics and issues in Christian theology. For quick reference and ease in studying, the works are written in a question and answer format. The questions follow a logical progression so that those reading straight through a work will receive a greater appreciation for the topic and the issues involved. The volumes are thorough, though not exhaustive, and can be used as a set or as single volume studies. Each volume is fully documented and contains a recommended reading list for those who want to pursue the subject in greater detail.

The study of theology and the many issues within Christianity is an exciting and rewarding endeavor. For two thousand years, Christians have proclaimed the gospel of Jesus Christ and sought to accurately define and defend the doctrines of their faith as recorded in the Bible. In 2 Timothy 2:15, Christians are exhorted: "Be diligent to present yourself approved to God as a workman who does not need to be ashamed, accurately handling the word of truth." The goal of these books is to help you in your diligence and accuracy as you study God's Word and its influence in history and thought through the centuries.

Introduction

Sometimes, the most significant news in the newspaper is found not on the front page or in the headlines but in the obituaries. If we have not already been notified by friends and loved ones, it is there that we learn of the death of friends, neighbors, and acquaintances. These brief lines and columns remind us of the brevity of life and the certainty of death. When we think about our own death or the death of a loved one or friend, theology becomes very personal.

In ages past, in the midst of suffering and death, Job asked, "If a man dies, will he live again?" (Job 14:14). Centuries passed before Jesus Christ provided the definitive answer to that question. He said in John 11:25–26, "I am the resurrection and the life; he who believes in Me will live even if he dies, and everyone who lives and believes in Me will never die." On the eve of His crucifixion, Jesus told the disciples, "In My Father's house are many dwelling places; if it were not so, I would have told you; for I go to prepare a place for you. If I go and prepare a place for you, I will come again and receive you to Myself; that where I am, there you may be also" (John 14:2–3).

The place of which Jesus spoke is heaven. It is the hope of all who believe in Him. Throughout the centuries, heaven has been depicted by artists and poets, authors and preachers, and many others seeking to give impressions and insights to their audiences. Augustine,

Dante, John Milton, John Bunyan, C. S. Lewis, and scores of others have written on heaven and its glories. It is sung about in hymns, spirituals, classical music, folk music, rock music, and country and western music. It is spoken of in jokes and in sermons, in hospitals and in classrooms. Almost everyone has some vague notions about it, some of them biblical and some of them unbiblical. The promise of heaven has brought hope to the weary, comfort to the grieving, and reassurance to those struggling in spiritual battles.

Heaven is very real. In an age of fantasy, special effects, mysticism, and spiritual apathy, it's easy for heaven to be misrepresented. Yet, the Bible is very clear about the existence and purpose of heaven. Heaven and the eternal state are part of God's plan for the ages; therefore, heaven and prophecy are integrally related.

What we believe about life and death, good and evil, and heaven and hell is most significant. C. S. Lewis wrote of heaven's importance, noting, "If you read history, you will find that the Christians who did most for the present world were just those who thought most of the next. . . . It is because Christians have largely ceased to think of the other world that they have become so ineffective in this one."[1] How true that is for all of us! When we think about heaven, it is of the utmost personal and theological significance.

Eschatology is the theological study of future events based upon Bible prophecy. All of the biblical prophecies regarding the future will be fulfilled according to God's plan and timing. Eschatology is about future events and personalities. It also relates to every person who has lived, is living, or will live. The Bible's teachings about heaven and hell relate to what we might term "personal eschatology." Heaven and hell are very real and very personal. They relate to your future.

Pastor and author Steven J. Lawson has written the following about heaven:

> Make no mistake about it, Heaven is a real place. It is not
> a state of mind. Not a figment of man's imagination. Not a

philosophical concept. Not a religious abstraction. Not a
sentimental dream. Not the medieval fancy of an ancient
scientist. Not the worn-out superstition of a liberal theologian. It's an actual place. A location far more real than
where you presently live. . . . It is a real place where God
lives. It is the real place from which Christ came into this
world. And it is the real place to which Christ returned at
His ascension—really![2]

The Bible doesn't tell us everything we would like to know about
heaven, but it does tell some things. It gives us glimpses of the future
to encourage us in the present. Let's see what the Bible teaches about
heaven—the glorious future that awaits all Christians.

Answers to Common Questions About Heaven and Eternity
is designed to provide readers a brief summary of this prophetic
topic. The theological perspective presented throughout this volume is that of premillennialism and pretribulationism. The authors
recognize that this view is not the only position embraced by evangelical Christians, but we believe that it is the most widely held and
prominent perspective. It is also our conviction that premillennialism, and specifically pretribulationism, best explains the prophetic
plan of God as revealed in the Bible. For those wishing to know
more about Bible prophecy, we encourage you to read our compan-
ion volume in this series, *Answers to Common Questions About the
End Times.*

PART 1

What Is Heaven?

1. Where does the Bible teach about heaven?

English translations of the Bible contain more than five hundred occurrences of the word *heaven*. Most of the verses use either the Hebrew word *shamayim*, which is literally translated "the heights," or the Greek word *ouranos*, which is literally translated "that which is raised up." These words are used throughout the Bible to refer to three different locations or realms: the atmosphere, the universe, and the abode of God. These three divisions have been recognized throughout history in both Christian and non-Christian sources, especially in classical Greek literature.[1] Although our concern is primarily the third usage, all three usages are common in the Bible.

The Atmospheric Heaven

Examples of this usage are seen in passages such as Deuteronomy 11:11, 17; 28:12, 24; Joshua 10:11; Psalms 18:13; 147:8; Proverbs 23:5; and Zechariah 2:6; 6:5. Verses such as these emphasize the "first heaven," or the atmospheric realm. It is of this realm that Isaiah speaks when he records God's words in Isaiah 55:9–11:

> For as the heavens are higher than the earth, so are My ways higher than your ways and My thoughts than your thoughts. For as the rain and the snow come down from

heaven, and do not return there without watering the earth and making it bear and sprout, and furnishing seed to the sower and bread to the eater; so will My word be which goes forth from My mouth; it will not return to Me empty, without accomplishing what I desire, and without succeeding in the matter for which I sent it.

The Universe, or Celestial Skies

Examples of this usage are seen in passages such as Genesis 1:14; 15:5; Exodus 20:4; Psalm 33:6; Jeremiah 10:2; and Hebrews 1:10. Frequently, the celestial skies or heavens are used biblically in figures of speech, such as a hyperbole (Deut. 1:28; Dan. 4:11, 20, 22), or a metonymy, which emphasizes totality (Deut. 4:39; 30:19; Matt. 24:31; Col. 1:23). It is of this realm of the celestial skies and the totality of the universe that we read in Deuteronomy 30:19: "I call heaven and earth to witness against you today, that I have set before you life and death, the blessing and the curse. So choose life in order that you may live, you and your descendants." It is also in this sense that we read of Jesus Christ's authority in Matthew 28:18–20:

> And Jesus came up and spoke to them, saying, "All authority has been given to Me in heaven and on earth. Go therefore and make disciples of all the nations, baptizing them in the name of the Father and the Son and the Holy Spirit, teaching them to observe all that I commanded you; and lo, I am with you always, even to the end of the age."

The Abode of God

Examples of this usage are the primary focus of this study and are seen in passages such as Psalm 33:13–14; Isaiah 63:15; Matthew 5:16, 45; 6:1, 9; 7:11, 21; 18:10; and Revelation 3:12; 21:10. It is the abode of God that Jesus spoke of when He stated in Matthew 10:32–33, "Therefore everyone therefore who confesses Me before men, I will also confess him before My Father who is in heaven.

But whoever denies Me before men, I will also deny him before My Father who is in heaven."

Jesus referred to heaven in this sense many times throughout His ministry. It is the abode of God, the "third heaven," of which Paul speaks in 2 Corinthians 12:2. It is also of this usage that Paul writes throughout his letters to the early churches.

Heaven is more than a mystical notion, an imaginary dreamland, or a philosophical concept. It is a real and present place in which God, the Creator of all things, lives. It is a place spoken of throughout the Bible. It is the true home of all Christians. It is where Jesus came from at the incarnation, where He ascended to after the resurrection, and from whence He will come again to receive all of those who truly follow Him. It is the place that the writer of Hebrews calls a "distant country" and for which those in his "hall of faith" longed:

> All these died in faith, without receiving the promises, but having seen them and having welcomed them from a distance, and having confessed that they were strangers and exiles on the earth. For those who say such things make it clear that they are seeking a country of their own. And indeed if they had been thinking of that country from which they went out, they would have had opportunity to return. But as it is, they desire a better country, that is, a heavenly one. Therefore God is not ashamed to be called their God; for He has prepared a city for them. (11:13–16)

2. Is there any difference between heaven and eternity?

When we talk about heaven, we are referring to a location or place. When we speak of eternity, we are talking about an era or eternal state. Heaven exists now even though we are not experiencing it. Eternity is a yet future dimension of time (without end). Heaven exists now and will continue to exist throughout eternity.

3. Where is heaven, and does it exist now?

The apostle Paul, writing to us as Christians in Philippians 3:20, declares "our citizenship is in heaven." Heaven is somewhere beyond earth and our universe. Heaven is in existence now and has been the dwelling place of God since eternity past. Heaven is the dwelling place of God, although God is not limited spatially to heaven because He is omnipresent. His omnipresence is reflected in Solomon's prayer at the dedication of the temple. "Behold, heaven and the highest heaven cannot contain You, how much less this house which I have built!" (1 Kings 8:27).

In Psalm 139:8, the psalmist also speaks of God's omnipresence, stating, "If I ascend to heaven, You are there; if I make my bed in Sheol, behold, You are there." God's omnipresence does not limit Him to heaven, but heaven is His habitation. John MacArthur writes,

> So to say that God dwells in heaven is not to say that He is contained there. But it is uniquely His home, His center of operations, His command post. It is the place where His throne resides. And it's where the most perfect worship of Him occurs. It is in that sense that we say heaven is His dwelling-place.[2]

Although heaven is a place, it is not limited by physical boundaries or boundaries of time and space. It can be experienced and inhabited by beings with material bodies, but it is not restricted to things such as height and width and breadth.[3] It has physical characteristics and attributes, but it is also extraphysical. MacArthur writes of heaven's attributes and uniqueness:

> So heaven is not confined to one locality marked off by boundaries that can be seen or measured. It transcends the confines of time-space dimensions. Perhaps that is part of what Scripture means when it states that God inhabits

eternity (Isa. 57:15). His dwelling place—heaven—is not subject to normal limitations of finite dimensions. We don't need to speculate about how this can be; it is sufficient to note that this is *how* Scripture describes heaven. It is a real place where people with physical bodies will dwell in God's presence for all eternity; and it is also a realm that surpasses our finite concept of what a "place" is.[4]

Although it is very real, heaven may be nonspatial in its present intermediate state. It is the place where Christ is now, but it is also beyond our normal senses and experiences. It is truly a supernatural phenomenon.[5]

4. When does the eternal state or eternity begin?

According to Revelation 21 and 22, the eternal state will begin at the end of the millennium, the thousand-year reign of Christ on earth. From our current point in history, the next event in God's prophetic plan is the rapture of the church, which will be followed by the seven-year tribulation, the second coming of Christ, the millennial kingdom, and, finally, the eternal state.

Eternity is distinct from the millennial kingdom. During the millennium, Jesus Christ will rule on earth for one thousand years. At the end of this period, there will be a series of judgments and the ushering in of the eternal state.

5. What is the eternal city?

After the judgments at the end of the millennium, Jerusalem and the rest of the earth will be destroyed by fire (Matt. 24:35; 2 Peter 3:10). However, according to Revelation 3:12 and 21–22, there will be a new city, the New Jerusalem, which will replace the destroyed city and which will continue throughout eternity. This new Jerusalem is the "eternal city" and part of heaven existing into eternity.[6]

Jesus told His disciples in John 14:2–3 that He was going away to heaven to prepare a place for believers. It appears that this place that He is preparing is the New, or heavenly, Jerusalem.

The New Jerusalem will be a heavenly city throughout eternity in that its origin is heavenly, as opposed to having been built upon this earth. However, it will be earthly, in that it will be physical and geographical, and it will be the earthly part of the new heavens and the new earth that will replace the current heavens and earth after their destruction. After this present earth has been destroyed by fire (2 Peter 3:10), then the new city will descend from the heavens. In Revelation, John states:

> Then I saw a new heaven and a new earth; for the first heaven and the first earth passed away, and there is no longer any sea. And I saw the holy city, new Jerusalem, coming down out of heaven from God, made ready as a bride adorned for her husband. And I heard a loud voice from the throne, saying, "Behold, the tabernacle of God is among men, and He will dwell among them, and they shall be His people, and God Himself will be among them." (Rev. 21:1–3)

Revelation 21 and 22 is very specific and detailed about the city, its inhabitants, and the blessedness of the eternal state. Biblical scholars and prophecy students disagree over the location of the heavenly Jerusalem during the millennium. Some believe that it will remain in heaven until the beginning of the eternal state. Others think that it will be present during the millennium, hovering above earthly Jerusalem and will be the abode of resurrected believers.

While most agree that Revelation 21 and 22 describes the heavenly Jerusalem, some interpret the passage as descriptive of Jerusalem during the millennium. Others see it as descriptive of the heavenly Jerusalem during the eternal state. There is also a mediating position which sees these chapters as describing the eternal habitation of resurrected saints during the millennium and continuing into the eternal state.

Following this mediating position, Dr. J. Dwight Pentecost writes:

> When the occupants of the city are described it must be seen that they are in their eternal state, possessing their eternal inheritance, in eternal relationship with God who has tabernacled among them. There will be no change in their position or relation whatsoever. When the occupants of the earth are described they are seen in the millennial age. They have an established relationship to the heavenly city which is above them, in whose light they walk. Yet their position is not eternal nor unchangeable, but rather millennial.[7]

Regardless of the view taken regarding the possibility of a "heavenly Jerusalem" that hovers over the earth during the millennium and in which those individuals with resurrection bodies dwell, Scripture is clear that there will be an earthly city of Jerusalem and a new heavenly Jerusalem. All scholars agree that both are a part of God's plan for history. Just when the heavenly Jerusalem will make its appearance in history is the question under discussion.

Although we might have many questions about eternity, John's vision leaves no doubt that citizens of this New Jerusalem, *the* eternal city, will exist in conditions unlike any that this world has known.

6. What is the relationship between the millennium and heaven?

The millennium and the eternal state are two separate phases of the kingdom of God. The millennium precedes the eternal state. Arnold Fruchtenbaum writes:

The millennium itself is only one thousand years long. However, according to the promises of the Davidic Covenant, there was to be an eternal dynasty, an eternal kingdom and an eternal throne. The eternal existence of the dynasty is assured because it culminates in an eternal person: the Lord Jesus Christ. But the eternal existence of the throne and kingdom must also be assured. The millennial form of the kingdom of God will end after one thousand years. But the kingdom of God in the sense of God's rule will continue into the Eternal Order. Christ will continue His position of authority on the Davidic throne into the Eternal Order.[8]

The millennium is the precursor of the eternal state. It will be different than life as we know it today, but it will still fall short of the absolute perfection of the eternal state. We read in Revelation 21–22:5 that the eternal state will entail the passing away of the old order and the arrival of the New Jerusalem and new heavens and earth.

When studying the two periods of time, we observe the following contrasts:

- The millennium is associated with the continuum of human history; the eternal state is not.
- The millennium is the apex of human history because sin is still present, though restrained through Christ's rule; heaven in the eternal state is totally void of all sin.
- The millennium will focus worship on Jesus Christ, the second person of the Trinity; during the eternal state, direct fellowship with God the Father, the first person of the Trinity, will be a reality for the first time in history since the fall.
- The millennium will be a time during which resurrected believers and nonresurrected humans will routinely commingle in history; the eternal state will consist of only resurrected believers.

- The millennium will still be a time in history when humans come into existence and will trust or reject Christ as their Savior; the eternal state will be a time during which no one else will ever be added to the human race and everyone's destiny will be frozen, locked into their condition as saved or lost for eternity.

The millennium and the eternal state will have many differences, but both of them will differ greatly from our current historical era.

7. What happens at the end of the millennium?

At the end of the thousand-year reign of Christ on earth, there will be one final rebellion by Satan and his forces. Just as is prophesied in Revelation 20, Satan will be loosed at the end of the millennium and will rebel against the millennial reign of Christ:

> When the thousand years are completed, Satan will be released from his prison, and will come out to deceive the nations which are in the four corners of the earth, Gog and Magog, to gather them together for the war; the number of them is like the sand of the seashore. And they came up on the broad plain of the earth and surrounded the camp of the saints and the beloved city, and fire came down from heaven and devoured them. And the devil who deceived them was thrown into the lake of fire and brimstone, where the beast and the false prophet are also; and they will be tormented day and night forever and ever. (Revelation 20:7–10)

In one final grasp for power and human allegiance, Satan will manifest his true nature (as he has done throughout all of history) and attempt to seize the throne of God.[9] John Walvoord writes of this attempted coup d'état:

The thousand years of confinement will not change Satan's nature, and he will attempt to take the place of God and receive the worship and obedience that is due God alone. He will find a ready response on the part of those who have made a profession of following Christ in the Millennium but who now show their true colors. They will surround Jerusalem in an attempt to capture the capital city of the kingdom of David as well as of the entire world. The Scriptures report briefly, "But fire came down from heaven and devoured them."[10]

According to Revelation 20:10, Satan's termination will be swift but everlasting. He will be cast into the lake of fire, joining the Antichrist and the False Prophet, who is the Antichrist's lieutenant (Rev. 13:11–18).

The fact that the Antichrist and the False Prophet are placed into the lake of fire at the second coming of Christ, before the millennium, demonstrates the fact that they are finished in history. The lake of fire is the final form of hell from which no one, once placed there, ever leaves. This is why Satan is bound in the bottomless pit at the start of the millennium, because he will make one more appearance upon the stage of history before he is once and for all consigned to the lake of fire.

The judgment of Satan is then followed by the judgment of the unbelieving dead, known as the great white throne judgment (Rev. 20:11–15). These judgments form the bridge between the millennium and the eternal state as described in Revelation 21–22. They are the final events of the millennium and conclude with the passing away of the present heavens and earth (Matt. 24:35; Mark 13:31; Luke 16:17; 21:33; 2 Peter 3:10). John writes: "Then I saw a new heaven and a new earth; for the first heaven and the first earth passed away, and there is no longer any sea" (Rev. 21:1).

8. How do the future judgments relate to heaven?

According to God's prophetic plan and timetable, several judgments are yet in the future. Some of these judgments will occur before and at the end of the tribulation, and others will come at the end of the millennium and before the eternal state. Just before the inauguration of the eternal state and the dwelling of believers in heaven for eternity, there will be the judgment of Satan and the fallen angels (Matt. 25:41; 2 Peter 2:4; Jude 6; Rev. 20:10) and the great white throne judgment of the unsaved that is described in Revelation 20:11–15. Charles Ryrie summarizes this final judgment thus:

> Those judged are simply called "the dead"—unbelievers (in contrast to "the dead in Christ" which refers to believers). This judgment will not separate believers from unbelievers, for all who will experience it will have made the choice during their lifetimes to reject God. The Book of Life which will be opened at the Great White Throne judgment will not contain the name of anyone who will be in that judgment. The books of works which will also be opened will prove that all who are being judged deserve eternal condemnation (and may be used to determine degrees of punishment). It is not that all their works were evil, but all were dead works, done by spiritually dead people. It is as if the Judge will say, "I will show you by the record of your own deeds that you deserve condemnation." So everyone who will appear in this judgment will be cast into the lake of fire forever.[11]

The various judgments are portrayed in the following chart.[12] Note that all of the judgments occur before the eternal state.

End-Time Judgments

Judgment	Time	Place	Persons	Basis	Results	Scripture
Believers' works	Between Rapture and Second Coming	*Bema* of Christ	Believers in Christ	Works and walk of the Christian life	Rewards or loss of rewards	1 Cor. 3:10–15; 2 Cor. 5:10
Old Testament saints	End of Tribulation/ Second Coming		Believers in Old Testament times	Faith in God	Rewards	Dan. 12:1–3
Tribulation saints	End of Tribulation/ Second Coming		Believers of Tribulation period	Faith in and faithfulness to Christ	Reign with Christ in the Millennium	Rev. 20:4–6
Living Jews	End of Tribulation/ Second Coming	Wilderness	Jews who survive the Tribulation	Faith in Christ	Believers enter kingdom; rebels are purged	Ezek. 20:34–38
Living Gentiles	End of Tribulation/ Second Coming	Valley of Jehoshaphat	Gentiles who survive the Tribulation	Faith in Christ as proved by works	Believers enter the kingdom; others go to lake of fire	Joel 3:1–2; Matt. 25:31–46
Satan and fallen angels	End of Millennium	Before the Great White Throne	Satan and those angels who follow him	Allegiance to Satan's counterfeit system	Lake of fire	Matt. 25:41; 2 Peter 2:4; Jude 6; Rev. 20:10
Unsaved people	End of Millennium		Unbelievers of all time	Rejection of God	Lake of fire	Rev. 20:11–15

PART 2

What Will Heaven Be Like?

9. What will take place in heaven?

The Bible describes life in heaven as full of joy, purposeful activity, and worship. When we think of eternity, it's easy to wonder if we will get bored in heaven. However, the biblical glimpses are not of boredom. The Bible speaks of at least six activities in heaven: worship, service, authority and administration, fellowship, learning, and rest.[1]

Worship Without Distraction

Worship will be the primary activity in heaven. As Wilbur Smith comments: "Perhaps the first great and continuous activity for the redeemed will be worship of the triune God."[2] Some of the most extensive passages on worship in heaven are found in Revelation 4–5 and 19:1–8.

Don Baker reflects on what worship in heaven will be like:

> Worship will no longer be an indefinable word or an indescribable experience. It will not be manipulated or contrived. All its pretense lost, worship will be one of the first and great continuous activities of the redeemed. It will be spontaneous and genuine. It will encompass the whole

universe. The hallelujahs and the praise the Lords and the amens will drown out all of the sounds of Heaven and earth, and we will all lose ourselves in the joy of telling our God how much we adore Him.[3]

On the basis of Revelation 4:8–11, the worship of God in heaven can be seen to include at least six things:[4]

1. A celebration of God's greatness (v. 8).
2. A celebration of God's goodness (v. 9).
3. A submission before God's sovereignty (v. 10).
4. An adoration of God's person (v. 10).
5. A self-renunciation before God's glory (v. 10).
6. An exaltation of God's name (v. 11).

Service Without Exhaustion

In Revelation 22:3 we read, "There will no longer be any curse; and the throne of God and of the Lamb will be in it, and His bondservants will serve Him." Throughout Revelation, the phrase *bondservant* is used to describe those who are in heaven and experiencing its glories. Unlike the current work, future service to God in heaven will be without time demands, without frustration, without fear of failure, without limitations, and without exhaustion. It will come from worship and motivation that is pure, and it will be a joyful experience.

Administration Without Failure

In Revelation 22:5, we read that believers in heaven shall "reign forever and ever." In Luke 19:17 and 19, Jesus taught that reward and authority would be given in the future to those who followed Him. He also indicated that the authority and administration would include judgment over the twelve tribes of Israel (Matt. 19:28; Luke 22:30). In 1 Corinthians 6:3, Paul states that Christians will also have authority over the angels in heaven.

Fellowship Without Suspicion

Heaven will provide believers of all ages with the opportunity for limitless fellowship with each other and with Jesus Christ (Matt. 8:11; Rev. 19:9). In heaven we will fellowship with those Christians we knew on earth, as well as Old Testament saints and those Christians who lived before and after us, or with those whom present circumstances have not allowed us to know.

Learning Without Weariness

Don Baker perfectly describes this aspect of heaven:

> We will not know everything in Heaven, for only God is omniscient, but will have a limitless capacity to learn. In the Fall, a curtain was lowered, which has caused us to "see through a glass darkly," but in Heaven that curtain will be lifted, and "I shall know, even as I am known" [1 Cor. 13:12]. One of the great joys of Heaven will be that of taking all the time necessary to unravel all the mysteries about God, about man, and about the universe.[5]

Rest Without Boredom

Revelation 14:10–13 contrasts the eternal destiny of the righteous and the unrighteous. In verse 11, the unrighteous are said to have "no rest" in contrast to the righteous, who will "rest from their labors, for their deeds follow with them" (v. 13). "A glorified spiritual body will know nothing of fatigue or exhaustion, so the continuing rest that God promises will not be a rest from work but a rest from want."[6] In heaven, we will be fully satisfied, and the words of David the psalmist will be fully realized by those who are God's own: "As for me, I shall behold Your face in righteousness; I will be satisfied with Your likeness when I awake" (Ps. 17:15).

10. Will we have bodies in heaven?

In heaven, we will have recognizable spiritual bodies just like

Jesus Christ had after the resurrection. In 1 John 3:2, the apostle John writes, "We know that when He appears, we will be like Him, because we will see Him just as He is." Earlier, in his gospel, John recorded Jesus' words regarding the resurrection of believers and the resurrection of judgment for unbelievers. He said, "An hour is coming, in which all who are in the tombs will hear His voice, and will come forth; those who did the good deeds to a resurrection of life, those who committed the evil deeds to a resurrection of judgment" (John 5:28–29).

The bodies that we will have in heaven will be our own earthly bodies glorified. They will have the same qualities as the glorified resurrection body of Jesus Christ. According to Philippians 3:21, Jesus Christ "will transform the body of our humble state into conformity with the body of His glory, by the exertion of the power that He has even to subject all things to Himself." In our resurrection bodies, the effects of the fall and of sin will be removed. The bodies will be real but without the physical limitations that we now experience and without the effects of disease, disability, or tragedy. Author and artist Joni Eareckson Tada, who became a quadriplegic after a diving accident as a teenager, writes of the certainty and glory of our resurrected bodies as described in 1 Corinthians 15:

> Somewhere in my broken, paralyzed body is the seed of what I shall become. The paralysis makes what I am to become all the more grand when you contrast atrophied, useless legs against splendorous resurrected legs. I'm convinced that if there are mirrors in heaven (and why not?), the image I'll see will be unmistakably "Joni," although a much better, brighter "Joni." So much so, that it's not worth comparing. . . . I will bear the likeness of Jesus, the man from heaven. Like His, mine will be an actual, literal body perfectly suited for earth and heaven. . . . We shall be perfectly fitted for our environment, whether it be the new heavens or new earth.[7]

All believers, regardless of the cause or nature of their death or the disposition of their remains at death, will miraculously receive new bodies. According to 1 Corinthians 15, our bodies will be imperishable, glorious, powerful, and spiritual. John MacArthur writes,

> All this is to say that in heaven we will have real bodies that are permanently and eternally perfect. You will never look in a mirror and notice wrinkles or a receding hairline. You will never have a day of sickness. You won't be susceptible to injury, or disease, or allergies. There will be none of those things in heaven. There will only be absolute, imperishable perfection.[8]

The doctrine of bodily resurrection and glorified bodies is essential to orthodoxy and the Christian message (1 Cor. 15:35–36). Based on the testimony and promises of the Bible, it is the great and glorious hope of Christians throughout all ages that they will one day be united with Jesus Christ in heavenly bodies. It is of this hope that Paul speaks in 1 Corinthians 15:12–19:

> Now if Christ is preached, that He has been raised from the dead, how do some among you say that there is no resurrection of the dead? But if there is no resurrection of the dead, not even Christ has been raised; and if Christ has not been raised, then our preaching is vain, your faith also is vain. Moreover we are even found to be false witnesses of God, because we testified against God that He raised Christ, whom He did not raise, if in fact the dead are not raised. For if the dead are not raised, not even Christ has been raised; and if Christ has not been raised, your faith is worthless; you are still in your sins. Then those also who have fallen asleep in Christ have perished. If we have hoped in Christ in this life only, we are of all men most to be pitied.

One thing that is not clear from the Bible is the apparent age of those in heaven. (This also relates to the issue of time in heaven.)[9] We know that there will be resurrection bodies, but we do not know what age they will appear. Will it be the appearance of a person's age at death or some other age (even if in life they did not reach that age)? This is a subject that theologians have discussed at least since the Middle Ages. Some, such as Thomas Aquinas, held that it would be about the age of thirty—when most people are at their peak physically and which is also near the age of Jesus when He died—but the question remains unanswered this side of heaven.[10]

11. Will we have personal identity in heaven?

Some religions teach that after death the soul of an individual merges with an impersonal Supreme Soul. However, the Bible teaches that there is and always will be—even in heaven—a distinct difference between human beings and God, who is infinite, personal, just, and loving. There will be personal identity in heaven. Jesus, in His resurrected body, ascended physically to heaven and will return in the same recognizable manner (Acts 1:9–11; Titus 2:13). Christians also will receive resurrection bodies that will be fully and completely transformed from what they were physically in this life (1 Cor. 15:12–57). Christian theology teaches that even those whose physical bodies have been destroyed by trauma or cremated will receive a perfect resurrection body.[11] When a Christian dies, he or she is consciously and immediately in the presence of Jesus Christ, our Savior in heaven (Luke 23:43; 2 Cor. 5:8). Although our bodies remain in the grave, our souls are immediately in God's presence, where we are conscious and awaiting resurrected bodies that will be attained at the rapture when Christ returns (1 Thess. 4:15–17; 1 John 3:2). Death does not eradicate identity.

12. Will we be able to recognize friends, loved ones, and others in heaven?

When we get to heaven, we will clearly recognize others. When

He was in His resurrection body, Jesus was clearly and readily recognized (except when He chose to conceal it when talking with the two on the road to Emmaus). In this same manner, we will be known and recognized by each other in heaven. We will not be nameless and faceless souls without identities. Rather, we will maintain our current identities but in resurrected and glorified bodies that have no infirmities or faults.

At the Last Supper, Jesus promised the disciples that in the millennial kingdom and in heaven they would all drink the fruit of the vine together again as they did that evening (Matt. 8:11; Luke 22:17–18). John MacArthur writes:

> All the redeemed will maintain their identity forever, but in a perfected form. We will be able to have fellowship with Enoch, Noah, Abraham, Jacob, Samuel, Moses, Joshua, Esther, Elijah, Elisha, Isaiah, Daniel, Ezekiel, David, Peter, Barnabas, Paul, or any of the saints we choose.
>
> Remember that Moses and Elijah appeared with Christ on the Mount of Transfiguration. Even though they died centuries before, they still maintained a clear identity (Matt. 17:3). Moreover, Peter, James, and John evidently recognized them (v. 4)—which implies that we will somehow be able to recognize people we've never even seen before. For that to be possible, we must all retain our individual identities, not turn into some sort of generic beings.[12]

The recognition, awareness, and knowledge of others will be enhanced rather than diminished or erased in heaven. Bible scholar Daniel Lockwood observes:

> Our resurrection bodies are not merely immortal duplicates of our present ones. Consider Paul's analogy of the wheat seed (1 Cor. 15:35–38). A mortal body is like the seed, while an immortal body is like the full-grown plant. Both

are physical, with an intrinsic continuity between the two. But what a difference between the seed and the plant in appearance, in attribute, and in potential! If we presently have the capacity to recognize our loves ones, that ability will be magnified, not lessened, in the immortal state.[13]

What the Bible does not tell us are the details of the resurrected and immortal body in heaven. Questions such as appearance of age and other attributes remain unanswered.

13. Will we be reunited with Christian family members and friends in heaven?

One of the greatest heartaches we face in this world is the longing and desire for loved ones and friends who are deceased. The desire to be with them and share our intimate concerns, thoughts, and wants is very real and strong. For Christians, such a reunion will happen in heaven and it will be an eternal reunion. Those whom we knew and loved for years or decades on earth will be with us for eternity.

In Psalm 116:15, we read, "Precious in the sight of the Lord is the death of His godly ones." God brings into His presence all of the redeemed, and each one is dear to Him, even more so than they are to us. We can be assured that in heaven we will know them, join them, and love them even more than we did here on earth. Although we might grieve for them now, we will not always, for God "will wipe away every tear from their eyes; and there will no longer be any death; there will no longer be any mourning, or crying, or pain; the first things have passed away" (Rev. 21:4).

Randy Alcorn astutely captures the issue of family members in heaven:

Heaven won't be without families but will be one big family, in which all family members are friends and all friends are family members. . . . Many of us treasure our families.

But many others have endured a lifetime of brokenheart-edness stemming from twisted family relationships. In Heaven, neither we nor our family members will cause pain. Our relationships will be harmonious—what we've longed for. . . . So, it's not at all true that there will be "no family in Heaven." On the contrary, there will be *one* great family—and none of us will ever be left out. Every time we see someone, it will be a family reunion.[14]

14. Is there marriage in heaven?

It is natural for us to wonder about the nature of our relationships with others in heaven, especially those who are close or intimate, such as families, dear friends, and spouses. The Bible clearly teaches that although our relationships will be perfect in heaven, there will be no marriage. In 1 Corinthians 7:29–31, the apostle Paul writes that the "form" (literally *schema* from the Greek) of this world is passing away. The relationships of this world and the way or manner of life, including marriage, will one day no longer exist.

But this I say, brethren, the time has been shortened, so that from now on those who have wives should be as though they had none; and those who weep, as though they did not weep; and those who rejoice, as though they did not rejoice; and those who buy, as though they did not possess; and those who use the world, as though they did not make full use of it; for the form of this world is passing away.

John MacArthur writes of this passage and our relationships in heaven:

Paul is not questioning the legitimacy of earthly blessings such as marriage, normal human emotions, and earthly ownership. But he is saying that we must never allow our emotions and possessions to control us so that we become entangled in this passing world. . . . Concentrate on the things of the Lord, because marriage is only a temporary provision.

If you're already married, however, this does not mean you may become indifferent to your marriage. Too much elsewhere in Scripture elevates the importance of marriage and commands husbands and wives to seek to honor God through the marriage relationship. But this passage simply underscores the temporal nature of marriage. While married couples are heirs together of the grace of this life (cf. 1 Peter 3:7), the institution of marriage is passing away. There are higher eternal values.[15]

When Jesus was asked about marriage in heaven and the afterlife, He taught that it was clearly a temporal union for this life. When some Sadducees, who did not believe in the afterlife, came to Him and asked Him a question in an attempt to force Him into taking sides with either them or the Pharisees (who believed we would have the same relationships in heaven as on earth), Jesus rebuked them sharply. After listening to their hypothetical scenario regarding marriage in this life and the afterlife, Jesus responded, "You are mistaken, not understanding the Scriptures nor the power of God. For in the resurrection they neither marry nor are given in marriage, but are like angels in heaven" (Matt. 22:29–30).

15. Are there animals in heaven?

Although at first glance this question might seem simplistic or foolish, it is a significant question that touches on many issues. The topic of animals in heaven relates to the doctrine of the existence of the soul, the doctrine of bodily resurrection, the purpose of all that is in creation, the extent of the fall, and distinctions between human beings and the rest of the creation. "Scripture says a great deal about animals, portraying them as Earth's second most important inhabitants. God entrusted animals to us, and our relationships with animals are a significant part of our lives."[16] In fact, through-out most of church history there has been the belief that animals had souls (though very different from human souls), even though animals were not created in God's image as were human beings and therefore were not equal to humans. It was only with the advent of the Enlightenment in the seventeenth century that their existence was questioned (along with the validity of the rest of Christian doctrine as well).[17]

We know from the Bible that there are definitely animals in the millennium prior to the eternal state, but the Bible is less clear about whether there will be animals in heaven. We also know that because animals are part of the created order, God the Father views them with pleasure and created them with care. Also, Jesus spoke of animals in terms showing their importance and frequently used them as illustrations in His teaching. The possibility of their presence in heaven is not a question to be lightly dismissed or ridiculed and it is one that has engaged Christian theologians since the earliest years of Christianity.[18] Animals certainly share in the effects of the fall of Adam and Eve and the consequences of original sin. Therefore, as part of the created order, they will experience the new order of the millennium (Ezek. 34:25-28; Hosea 2:18; Zech. 2:4).

Ever since the fall of Adam and Eve in the garden of Eden, humanity and creation have been under the judgment and ramifications of their original sin. The pollution of sin has affected all of humanity and all of creation. The Apostle Paul reminds us of what we experience daily when he declares in Romans 8:22, "For we know that the whole creation groans and suffers the pains of child-birth together until now." However, during the millennium there will be a partial lifting of the curse and ramifications of original sin. There will still be death and the complete effects of the fall will not be lifted until the creation of the new heaven and new earth in the eternal state after the millennium (Rev. 22:3).

The millennial kingdom will bring about harmony in all of creation. Some of the most graphic portrayals of the millennial kingdom are found in the prophecies of Isaiah. In chapters 11 and 35, Isaiah provides extensive comment on the physical aspects of the kingdom.

In Isaiah 35:1–2, we read of some of the effects of the millennium on the environment:

> The wilderness and the desert will be glad, and the Arabah will rejoice and blossom; like the crocus it will blossom profusely and rejoice with rejoicing and shout of joy. The glory of Lebanon will be given to it, the majesty of Carmel and Sharon. They will see the glory of the LORD, the majesty of our God.

There will be abundant rainfall in areas that are currently known for their dryness; therefore, there will be plenty of food for animals.

> Then He will give you rain for the seed which you will sow in the ground, and bread from the yield of the ground, and it will be rich and plenteous; on that day your livestock will graze in a roomy pasture. Also the oxen and the donkeys which work the ground will eat salted fodder, which has been winnowed with shovel and fork. (Isa. 30:23–24)

> The scorched land will become a pool and the thirsty ground springs of water; in the haunt of jackals, its resting place, grass becomes reeds and rushes. (Isa. 35:7)

As part of nature and the created order, animal life will also be affected. The predatory instincts and carnivorous appetites will cease in animals. The distinctions between "tame" and "wild" will be eradicated and all creatures will live in harmony.

> And the wolf will dwell with the lamb, and the leopard will lie down with the young goat, and the calf and the young

lion and the fatling together; and a little boy will lead them. Also the cow and the bear will graze; their young will lie down together; and the lion will eat straw like the ox. (Isa. 11:6–7)

In Revelation 21:5, Christ proclaims from His throne in the New Heaven, "Behold, I am making all things new." There is no reason to believe that this excludes the animal kingdom, especially when this verse is considered with other passages such as Romans 8:21–23.[19]

16. How do angels relate to heaven and eternity?

Angels are very real. They exist and minister today just as they have in the past, and they will continue to exist in heaven and eternity.[20] Theologian and Bible scholar Charles Ryrie writes of angels:

If one accepts the biblical revelation then there can be no question about the existence of angels. There are three significant characteristics about revelation. First, it is extensive. The Old Testament speaks about angels just over 100 times, while the New Testament mentions them about 165 times. . . .

Second, angels are mentioned throughout the Bible. The truth about them is not confined to one period of history or one part of the Scriptures or a few writers. They do not belong to some primitive era. Their existence is mentioned in thirty-four books of the Bible from the earliest (whether Gen. or Job) to the last.

Third, the teaching of our Lord includes a number of references to angels as real beings. So to deny their existence is to cast doubt on His veracity.[21]

Angels are created spiritual beings (Ps. 148:5) that do not procreate (Matt. 22:30) and that function as messengers and servants of God (Heb. 1:14). It is important to remember that angels and humans are both created, but very distinct from each other. Humans do not become angels in heaven. Angels serve as God's agents on earth and in heaven, but their purpose is very different from humans.[22]

Angels will participate in the prophetic events before the eternal state. Just as they were present at Christ's first coming, so also will they be present at the rapture (1 Thess. 4:16), during the tribulation (Rev. 8–9; 16), at the second coming (Matt. 25:31; 2 Thess. 1:7), and at the final judgment (Matt. 13:39–40).

Angels will be present in heaven and eternity and Christians will judge them because of our union with Christ. In 1 Corinthians 6:3, Paul tells the Corinthians, "Do you not know that we will judge the angels?" We also know from passages such as 2 Peter 2:4 and Jude 6 that the fallen angels who sided with Satan when he rebelled against God will be judged in the future and cast into hell with him.

PART 3

Who Will Be in Heaven?

17. Who are the occupants of heaven?

In heaven there now is and will be God, angels, and redeemed believers.

- God. Heaven is God's dwelling place. Psalm 103:19 says, "The LORD has established His throne in the heavens, and His sovereignty rules over all."
- Angels. Angels are given assignments throughout the universe and have access to heaven and earth, but their home is in heaven (Isa. 6:1–6; Dan. 7:10; Mark 13:32; John 1:51).
- Believers. All Christians of all ages, along with the redeemed of the Old Testament era, will have their eternal home in heaven (Rev. 5:9). Philippians 3:20 states, "For our citizenship is in heaven, from which also we eagerly wait for a Savior, the Lord Jesus Christ."

Heaven will be filled eternally with those who know and love God. It will be a place of praise and worship, joy and gladness. The trials and tribulations of this world will be gone, and the true citizenship of Christians will be fully realized. John recorded a preview of heaven, God's "coming attraction," in the book of Revelation. We read there of heaven's occupants:

After these things I looked, and behold, a great multi-
tude, which no one could count, from every nation and
all tribes and peoples and tongues, standing before the
throne and before the Lamb, clothed in white robes, and
palm branches were in their hands; and they cry out with
a loud voice, saying, "Salvation to our God who sits on the
throne, and to the Lamb." And all the angels were standing around the throne and around the elders and the four
living creatures; and they fell on their faces before the
throne and worshipped God, saying, "Amen, blessing and
glory and wisdom and thanksgiving and honor and power
and might, be to our God forever and ever, Amen." (Rev.
7:9–12)

18. What happens now at the moment of death?

When a Christian dies, his or her spirit is immediately brought
into heaven and the eternal presence of God. The Bible clearly
teaches that when Christians die, they are instantaneously present with God. In Philippians 1:23, Paul writes, "But I am hard-
pressed from both directions, having the desire to depart and be
with Christ, for that is very much better." Notice that there is no
indication of any time lapse in his comment. This is stated even
stronger in 2 Corinthians 5:6–8, where he writes, "Therefore,
being always of good courage, and knowing that while we are
at home in the body we are absent from the Lord—for we walk
by faith, not by sight—we are of good courage, I say, and prefer
rather to be absent from the body and to be at home with the
Lord." Hebrews 12:23 also suggests that believers who have died
are now in heaven without their resurrected bodies, awaiting the
time when the body and the soul will be united in a final glorified state.

Jesus clearly promised the thief who was crucified beside Him
that they would be together in paradise at the same moment and
day (Luke 23:43). In Revelation 6:9–11, John writes of the souls

of disembodied spirits martyred during the early days of the Tribulation crying out for divine justice. These verses show a consciousness of believers and their presence with God. John MacArthur writes of the death of believers:

> God made man body and soul—we consist of an inner man and an outer man (Gen. 2:7). Therefore our ultimate perfection demands that both body and soul be renewed. Even the creation of a new heaven and new earth demands that we have bodies—a real earth calls for its inhabitants to have real bodies. . . . Death results in separation of the body and the soul. Our bodies go to the grave, and our spirits go to the Lord. The separation continues until the resurrection: "The hour is coming, in which all that are in the graves shall hear his voice, and shall come forth; they that have done good, unto the resurrection of life; and they that have done evil, unto the resurrection of damnation" (John 5:28–29 KJV). Right now the souls of believers who have died are in heaven. But someday their bodies will be resurrected and joined to their spirits, and they will enjoy the eternal perfection of body and soul.[1]

Revelation 6:9-11 also makes it clear that Christians are conscious with Jesus after death. "There the souls of tribulation martyrs in heaven ask the Lord how long it will be until their righteous blood is avenged. Apparently without resurrected bodies yet, they are still fully conscious, having speech and recollection."[2]

Unbelievers are not and will not be in heaven. At the time of death, an unbeliever's body enters the grave, and the soul of the unbeliever enters hades to wait for the final judgment at the end of the millennium. Like a believer's body, the unbeliever's body will one day be joined with their souls. But this resurrection will be for final judgment, and they will not receive glorified bodies.

19. What about the concept of soul sleep?

Some groups, such as Seventh-day Adventists and the Jehovah's Witnesses, teach a concept of soul sleep. This view holds that between death and resurrection a person enters an unconsciousness or sleep. The concept is based on the fact that several passages in the Bible refer to death as "sleep" (Dan. 12:2; Matt. 9:24; John 11:11; 1 Thess. 4:13–16; 5:10). We have, however, several biblical and theological objections to this doctrine and to taking these passages as referring to soul sleep.[3]

- Several passages—including Luke 23:43; 2 Corinthians 5:1–10; and Philippians 1:23—teach that death for the believer is an immediate transition into conscious enjoyment of the presence of Christ. This situation could not be so if they were in soul sleep.
- Some of these same passages refer to death as a gain because the deceased is immediately with Christ. If the believer were in soul sleep, it would not be a gain.
- In 1 Thessalonians 5:10, Paul writes, "[Christ] died for us, so that whether we are awake or asleep, we will live together with Him." If being "asleep" here means soul sleep, then the verse makes no sense; we would not then "live together with Him."
- Because sleep is an activity of the body, the soul sleeps now only because it is embodied. Once the body and the soul are separated at death, it is unclear how a disembodied soul could or would need to have rest.
- The existence of angels is proof that spirits can and do exist and have conscious, disembodied lives. Therefore, no problem exists with the concept of a conscious, disembodied intermediate state for human beings.
- The history and usage of the word *sleep* in the ancient Near Eastern, Egyptian, and Greek cultures makes arguing for soul sleep difficult because the word commonly described the appearance and posture of the body, not the soul.

Soul sleep is not a biblical doctrine, and it adds confusion to the prophetic teachings of the Bible. If soul sleep is true, then we must cast aside Scripture because we cannot, as Paul teaches, "prefer rather to be absent from the body and to be at home with the Lord" (2 Cor. 5:8).

20. Who enters heaven?

Heaven is for all those who have obtained salvation based on the death of Jesus Christ. As we have seen from the preceding questions, the souls of all believers enter heaven at the moment of death. There they await, with the Old Testament saints, their glorified resurrection bodies.

People long to live life to its fullest; yet, for Christians "the fullest" will come only after death. It will come in heaven when we see our Creator and Lord face to face and are finally and eternally "home." Ken Gire has written of our frequent misperception of death: "Death. It is the most misunderstood part of life. It is not a great sleep but a great awakening. It is that moment when we awake, rub our eyes, and see things at last the way God has seen them all along."[4]

21. What happens when infants, children, and others who can't believe in Jesus Christ die?

This issue is certainly one of the most personal, emotional, and difficult questions we face as Christians. Many people, because of diminished mental capacities or because they die as infants or young children, do not have the opportunity to respond to the offer of salvation through Jesus Christ. The Bible does not give us all of the clarity or intricacy of response that we desire in answers regarding their destiny, but it does give some assurance to us and provides several insights.

When King David's very young son died, David mourned his death but firmly believed that he would one day be reunited with his son in heaven. We read David's words in 2 Samuel 12:22–23:

"While the child was still alive, I fasted and wept; for I said, 'Who knows, the LORD may be gracious to me, that the child may live.' But now he has died; why should I fast? Can I bring him back again? I will go to him, but he will not return to me." David knew that death was inevitable, but he fully expected to be reunited with his son after death.

In Matthew 18:1–6, 10–14, and 19:14, Jesus speaks with extreme gentleness and favor regarding children and the kingdom of God. On the basis of these and other passages, the majority of Christian theologians have held to salvation for those such as infants who can't believe in Christ's redeeming work. Representative of this perspective, Ron Rhodes writes:

> It would be a cruel mockery for God to call upon infants to do—and to hold them responsible for doing—what they could not do. At a young age children simply do not have the capacity to exercise saving faith in Christ.
>
> I believe it is the uniform testimony of Scripture that those who are not capable of making a decision to receive Jesus Christ, when they die, go to be with Christ in heaven, resting in His tender arms, enjoying the sweetness of His love.[5]

The view presented by Rhodes and many others is that if an individual dies before he or she reaches an age or capacity for moral accountability, the individual is granted salvation at the moment of death. In James 4:17, we read, "Therefore, to one who knows the right thing to do, and does not do it, to him it is sin." Rhodes writes, "It would seem, then, that when a child truly comes into a full awareness and moral understanding of 'oughts' and 'shoulds,' he or she at that point has reached the age of accountability."[6] He continues,

> Even though the child does not become morally responsible before God until this time, he or she nevertheless has a sin nature that alienates him or her from God from the

moment of birth. And whatever solution a person comes up with in regard to the issue of infant salvation must deal with this problem.

The solution, it seems to me, must be that at the moment the infant dies—and not before—the benefits of Jesus' atoning death on the cross are applied to him or her. And at that moment, the infant becomes saved and is immediately brought into the presence of God in heaven. This view is consistent not just with the love of God, but His holiness as well.[7]

Another passage used in support of the concept of the age of accountability is Revelation 20:12–13, which states that the final judgment of the wicked is "according to their deeds." Rhodes writes, "The basis of this judgment of the wicked is clearly deeds done while on earth. Hence, infants and mentally handicapped people cannot possibly be the objects of this judgment because they are not responsible for their deeds. Such a judgment against infants would be a travesty."[8]

The age of accountability is considered to extend to preborn babies as well as infants and others.[9] We know with absolute certainty that God's attributes include absolute love, justice, and goodness (Pss. 31:19; 103:6, 8–10; Nah. 1:7; Zeph. 3:5; 1 John 4:16). For those who grieve or have grieved the loss of a child or questioned the destiny of another person who is or was unable to believe, we are assured that they are more precious to God than we can imagine. He knows our fears and sees our tears and will not permit any individual or group of individuals to perish without the willful choice of that individual. Evangelical theologian Robert Lightner has written appropriately, "How would God be just in refusing into His presence those who were never able to receive or reject His salvation?"[10]

22. How does Jesus Christ relate to heaven?

Forty days after the Resurrection, Jesus entered heaven, and He will remain there until the rapture (Acts 1:9–11; 1 Thess. 4:16–17).

Before His crucifixion, Jesus had told the disciples that He would return to heaven to prepare an eternal home for those who believed in Him. In John 14:1–3, He said:

> Do not let your heart be troubled; believe in God, believe also in Me. In My Father's house are many dwelling places; if it were not so, I would have told you; for I go to prepare a place for you. And if I go and prepare a place for you, I will come again and receive you to Myself; that where I am, there you may be also.

Believers will enjoy eternal fellowship with Jesus Christ in heaven. "Christ is the centerpiece of Heaven. All Heaven revolves around Him."[11] We will see, experience, and understand in heaven all of the glory and majesty of Christ. John MacArthur writes:

> Simply put, we're going to be with a Person as much as we are going to live in a place. The presence of Christ is what makes heaven. "The Lamb is the light thereof" (Rev. 21:23 KJV). And perfect fellowship with God is the very essence of heaven.[12]

PART 4

What Does the Future Hold for Non-Christians?

23. Doesn't everyone go to heaven?

We often hear the phrase "there are many paths to the mountaintop," implying that either all religions have equally valid claims to truth or that all of humanity will ultimately experience the same final disposition. Within Christianity, some people have claimed that everyone will receive salvation. Yet, this position of inclusivism does not have the support of the Bible and has not been the historic position of Christian orthodoxy. Passages such as Matthew 25:46, John 3:36, 2 Thessalonians 1:8–9, and numerous others clearly teach that salvation will not be experienced by everyone.[1] This is, admittedly, a difficult and emotional issue. It should, however, be a motivating factor for every Christian to share his or her faith. It is a very important matter, for eternity rests in the balance.

24. What is hell?

Hell is a place of eternal punishment and separation from God. It was created to accommodate Satan and the fallen angels who rebelled with him against God (Matt. 25:41). People who reject Jesus Christ and His free offer of salvation will join Satan in hell in eternity. Hell is a very real place of literal fire and flames, but the most important thing to know about it is that hell is separation from God. It is what people choose rather than accepting salvation through Jesus Christ. Theologian Harold O. J. Brown commented appropriately that "Hell has been called 'the most enduring monument to the freedom of the will.'"[2] Similarly, C. S. Lewis wrote, "There are only two kinds of people in the end: those who say to God, 'Thy will be done,' and those to whom God says, '*Thy* will be done.'"[3]

The concept of hell and belief in it is not popular in our society, but hell is a valid biblical doctrine. Theologians and apologists Gary Habermas and J. P. Moreland summarize hell very well:

> Hell is a place of shame, sorrow, regret, and anguish. This intense pain is not actively produced by God; he is not a cosmic torturer. Undoubtedly, anguish and torment will exist in hell. And because we will have both body and soul in the resurrected state, the anguish experienced can be both mental and physical. But the pain suffered will be due to the shame and sorrow resulting from the punishment of final, ultimate, unending banishment from God, his kingdom, and the good life for which we were created in the first place. Hell's occupants will deeply and tragically regret all they lost. As Jesus said, "For what profit is it to a man if he gains the whole world, and loses his own soul?" (Matt. 16:26 NKJV).[4]

25. Where does the Bible teach about hell?

The Bible refers to hell using several different words throughout the Old and New Testaments. Two of the clearest passages on hell in the New Testament are 2 Thessalonians 1:9 and Matthew 25:41, 46. In 2 Thessalonians 1:9, Paul writes of those who reject God: "These will pay the penalty of eternal destruction, away from the presence of the Lord and from the glory of His power." Matthew's gospel records Jesus' words about future judgment and hell:

> Then He will also say to those on His left, 'Depart from Me, accursed ones, into the eternal fire which has been prepared for the devil and his angels. . . . These will go away into eternal punishment, but the righteous into eternal life. (25:41, 46)

Following is a brief summary of the biblical words from which we get the English word *hell*.

Sheol

In the Old Testament, the Hebrew word *sheol* is used to describe hell. It occurs sixty-five times and is translated by terms such as *hell, pit, grave,* and *sheol. Sheol* can have different meanings in different contexts in the Bible. It may refer to the grave (Job 17:13; Ps. 16:10; Isa. 38:10). It also means the place to which the departed go (Gen. 37:35; 42:38; Num. 16:33; Job 14:13; Ps. 55:15). Believers will be rescued from *sheol* (Pss. 16:9–11; 17:15; 49:15), but the wicked will not (Job 21:13; 24:19; Pss. 9:17; 31:17; 49:14; 55:15). The major focus of the Old Testament is on the place where the bodies of people go after death, not where their souls exist. The destiny of the souls of individuals in the intermediate state is not expanded upon greatly in the Old Testament. The full doctrine of eternal destiny must be rounded out with the revelation of the New Testament. But *sheol* is definitely a place of punishment (Job 24:19; Ps. 30:9).

Hades

The New Testament Greek counterpart to the Hebrew term *sheol* is *hades. Hades* was originally a proper noun in Greek, the name of the Greek god of the netherworld who ruled over the dead. In the New Testament, the term *hades* is used in two different ways. First, it can be used to describe a place when referring to punishment (Matt. 11:23; Luke 10:15; 16:23). Second, it can refer to the state of death that everyone experiences at the end of life (Matt. 16:18; Acts

2:27, 31; Rev. 1:18; 6:8; 20:13–14). Hades is a temporary location. Its occupants will eventually be cast into the lake of fire after the great white throne judgment.

Gehenna

This word is used twelve times in the New Testament and is a term for eternal punishment. The term is derived from the Hebrew word referring to the Valley of Hinnon that runs on the southern and eastern sides of Jerusalem. In Old Testament times, the valley was a place in which pagan worshipers sacrificed infants by fire to the false god Moloch (2 Kings 16:3; 17:17; 21:6). Jeremiah also announced that the valley would be a place of divine judgment (Jer. 7:32; 19:6). In New Testament times, the valley became a place where refuse was continually burned. The imagery of the word *gehenna* would have been very vivid for the New Testament audience. Therefore, the word became synonymous with eternal punishment and the fires of hell. Its usage describes the eternal punishment associated with the final judgment (Matt. 23:15, 33; 25:41, 46).

Tartaros

This term occurs only in 2 Peter 2:4 and refers to a place where certain, not all, fallen angels (demons) are confined. The word was used in classical mythology for a subterranean abyss in which rebellious gods were punished. The word came over into Hellenistic Judaism and was used also in the apocryphal book of Enoch (2:20) in reference to fallen angels.

Other descriptions

Several other phrases or descriptions of eternal punishment are found in the New Testament, among them are: *unquenchable fire* (Matt. 3:12; Mark 9:43, 48); *furnace of fire* (Matt. 13:42, 50); *outer darkness* (Matt. 8:12; 22:13; 25:30); *eternal fire* (Matt. 25:41); and *lake of fire* (Rev. 19:20; 20:10, 14–15).

26. Will the punishment in hell be eternal?

According to Revelation 20:11–15, unbelievers will be cast into the lake of fire (hell) after the great white throne judgment, and they will remain there for eternity. It is an individual's own choice that brings about this eternal punishment. Habermas and Moreland comment: "Unquestionably the greatest pain suffered by people in hell is that they are forever excluded from the presence of God. If ecstatic joy is found in the presence of God (Ps. 16:11), then utter dismay is found in His absence."[5] Every person must decide if he or she will spend eternity in heaven or in hell. The choice is either eternal punishment or eternal life (Matt. 25:46).

27. What is purgatory?

One of the doctrines that has separated Protestants from Roman Catholics since the Reformation in the 1500s is the Roman Catholic belief in purgatory—a transitional process and state of final purification into which the dead who are assured of salvation enter for an unspecified time before finally entering heaven. Though it is often thought of as a place, official Roman Catholic teaching does not argue for such a thing.

It was the teaching and doctrine of purgatory that was the immediate occasion of Martin Luther's 1517 revolt against the selling of indulgences (full or partial remission of temporal punishment for sins already forgiven once the sinner has confessed and received absolution) by Johann Tetzel, a Dominican preacher acting on behalf of the Archbishop of Mainz.

The word *purgatory* was first used in the twelfth century and comes from the Latin verb *purgare* ("to purge") and the Latin *purgatorium,* which was used to refer to the process of purification. The idea of purgatory as a place also emerged in the twelfth century, probably between 1150 and 1200.[6] The doctrine of purgatory was first articulated in the medieval era at the Second Council of Lyon (1274) and the Council of Florence (1438–1445), and then reiterated during the Reformation era at the Council of Trent (1545–1563).

Roman Catholic teaching as found in the *Compendium of the Catechism of the Catholic Church* (2005), which is a summary of the 1992 *Catechism of the Catholic Church,* states of the following:

> 210. What is purgatory?
> Purgatory is the state of those who die in God's friendship, assured of their eternal salvation, but who still have need of purification to enter into the happiness of heaven.
>
> 211. How can we help the souls being purified in purgatory?
> Because of the communion of saints, the faithful who are still pilgrims on earth are able to help the souls in purgatory by offering prayers in suffrage for them, especially the Eucharistic sacrifice. They also help them by almsgiving, indulgences, and works of penance.[7]

In Roman Catholic teaching, purgatory is considered a "third state" between heaven and hell. Each person undergoes immediate judgment after death at which time the soul's eternal destiny is determined. Some are immediately united with God in heaven, some are immediately destined for hell, and some undergo the purification of purgatory. These are believed to be souls that are not sufficiently free from the temporal effects of sin: "All who die in God's grace and friendship, but still imperfectly purified, are indeed assured of their eternal salvation; but after death they undergo purification, so as to achieve the holiness necessary to enter the joy of heaven."[8]

One of the presuppositions underlying Roman Catholic belief in purgatory is the distinction between mortal sin and venial sin (a distinction not made in Protestantism). Mortal sin causes eternal loss of the soul in hell, whereas venial sin does not cause eternal damnation. Catholic teaching states that venial sins that an individual commits and for which he or she does not achieve purification in the present life may be purified after death in purgatory.

Also closely tied to belief in purgatory is the practice of praying for the dead. This practice is supported by a verse from the Apocrypha (writings not accepted by Protestants as part of the canon of the Bible):

> This teaching is also based on the practice of prayer for the dead, already mentioned in Sacred Scripture: "Therefore [Judas Maccabeus] made atonement for the dead, that they might be delivered from their sin" [2 Maccabees 12:46] From the beginning the Church has honored the memory of the dead and offered prayers in suffrage for them, above all the Eucharistic sacrifice, so that, thus purified, they may attain the beatific vision of God. The Church also commends almsgiving, indulgences, and works of penance undertaken on behalf of the dead.[9]

Eastern Orthodoxy does not argue for the existence of purgatory even though it believes that there is a judgment immediately after death. However, in Eastern Orthodox teaching, the dead do not receive either final bliss in heaven or damnation in hell until the final judgment at the end of time. As in Roman Catholicism, Eastern Orthodoxy teaches that prayers prayed on their behalf by the living can aid the souls of the deceased.

In literature and popular culture it was the writing of the Italian poet Dante Alighieri (1265–1321) who shaped western conceptions of purgatory in the *Divine Comedy* and "carved out for it an enduring place in human memory."[10] The idea of purgatory was rejected by the Protestant Reformers and both Martin Luther and John Calvin wrote against it.[11]

28. Is there any biblical evidence for purgatory?

Purgatory is not mentioned in the Bible. Roman Catholic support for prayers for the dead and indulgences includes 2 Maccabees

12:42–46 (from the Apocrypha) and interpretations of Matthew
12:32, 1 Corinthians 3:10–15, and 2 Timothy 1:18. The *New Catholic
Encyclopedia* states: "In the final analysis, the Catholic doctrine on
purgatory is based on tradition, not Sacred Scripture."[12]

29. What is Limbo?

In the past, in official Roman Catholic teaching, Limbo was
a state or place of existence for infants who died without being
baptized and without receiving salvation. The word comes from
the Latin *limbus,* meaning "hem of the border" as of a garment.
Because of the Roman Catholic belief in baptismal regeneration,
it was thought essential to have baptism in order to have salvation.
Because infants had original sin but not personal sin, the question
arose regarding what happened to them if they died before they
were baptized. It was thought that the unbaptized infant did not
merit hell but also could not enter heaven.

The idea was not present in the patristic era of Christianity
and arose in the thirteenth century with the writings of Thomas
Aquinas. Aquinas held that unbaptized infants who die enjoy a
natural bliss. The idea was disputed in Roman Catholic theology
for centuries and the only official document containing the word
Limbo is the decree *Auctorem Fidei* (1794). According to the *New
Catholic Encyclopedia*, "From the history of this document it is
certain that the Church merely wished to defend the common
teaching from slander. As such it is not a defense of the existence
of Limbo."[13] The idea of Limbo was never uniformly taught and
accepted in Roman Catholicism, although there was wide popular belief in it. The idea is not taught today in official Roman
Catholic dogma. "Most theologians today regard the 'limbo of
children' as a once-popular, but now inert, theological opinion
that attempted to resolve the theological tension between the
Church's teaching on the necessity of baptism for salvation and
the acknowledgment that infants and young children are inno-
cent of personal sin."[14]

30. Is there any biblical evidence for Limbo?

The concept of Limbo does not appear in the Bible or even in the first centuries of the history of the church. The teaching arose during the thirteenth century, especially in the teachings of Thomas Aquinas (ca. 1224–1274).

31. What about annihilationism?

Some evangelicals advocate the position of annihilationism or conditional immortality. Sometimes the two terms have different nuances; at other times, they have the same meaning. Gary Habermas and J. P. Moreland note,

> When used differently, conditional immortality is the notion that humans are by nature mortal, God gives the gift of everlasting life to believers, and at death God simply allows unbelievers to become extinct. Annihilationism often refers to the view that everyone survives death and participates in the final resurrection, but the judgment passed on unbelievers is extinction. Non-Christians undergo everlasting punishment, not everlasting punishing, in that the result of their judgment—annihilation—lasts forever.[15]

We have several arguments against annihilationism, the strongest of which is the fact that many biblical passages refute it (Matt. 25:41, 46; Mark 9:48; Rev. 14:9-11; 20:10).[16] We have noted earlier Jesus' words in Matthew 25:46, Jesus clearly taught that the consequences of rejecting Him were eternal: "These will go away into eternal punishment, but the righteous into eternal life" (Matt. 25:46). Ron Rhodes writes of this passage:

> By no stretch of the imagination can the punishment spoken of in Matthew 25:46 be defined as a nonsuffering extinction of consciousness. Indeed, if actual suffering is lacking, then so is punishment. Let us be clear on this:

punishment entails suffering. And suffering necessarily entails consciousness. . . . A critical point to make about the punishment described in Matthew 25:46 is that it is said to be eternal. There is no way that annihilationism or an extinction of consciousness can be forced into that passage. Indeed, the Greek adjective aionion in that verse literally means "everlasting, without end." . . . This same adjective is predicated of God (the "eternal" God) in 1 Timothy 1:17, Romans 16:26, Hebrews 9:14, 13:8, and Revelation 4:9. The punishment of the wicked is just as eternal as our eternal God.[17]

32. What about universalism?

Universalism is the belief that all men and women of all ages will ultimately receive salvation and spend eternity in heaven. Universalism has been found in Christianity throughout the centuries, but it has never been considered orthodox, nor has it been widely accepted. Advocates of universalism claim that eternal punishment is inconsistent with a loving God. This view, however, minimizes the justice of God.

Dr. Ryrie responds to the theological argument of a loving God:

Some universalists prefer to argue theologically. They appeal to the nature of God as being totally love. How then, they ask, could such a God condemn anyone either in this life or the life to come? God is too good to reject anyone. However God's character involves not only love and goodness but also righteousness, holiness, and wrath. Universalists sacrifice God's righteousness to His love which results in a god different from the God of the Bible.

Others argue that a just God would not give infinite punishment for finite sin. But this ignores that important principle that crime depends on the object against whom it is committed (an infinite God) as well as on the subject who commits it (finite man). Striking a post is not a culpable act as striking a human being is. All sin is ultimately against an infinite God and deserves infinite punishment.[18]

Ron Rhodes writes of universalism:

The older form of universalism, originating in the second century, taught that salvation would come after a temporary period of punishment. The newer form of universalism declares that all men are now saved, though all do not realize it. Therefore the job of the preacher and the missionary is to tell people they are already saved. Certain Bible passages—John 12:32, Philippians 2:10–11, and 1 Timothy 2:4—are typically twisted out of context in support of universalism.[19]

The Bible is very clear on the fact that not all people will receive salvation and spend eternity in heaven. John 3:18 states, "He who believes in Him is not judged; he who does not believe has been judged already, because he has not believed in the name of the only begotten Son of God." Later in the same chapter we read, "He who believes in the Son has eternal life; but he who does not obey the Son will not see life, but the wrath of God abides on him" (v. 36).

33. What about reincarnation?

Reincarnation, also known as transmigration of the soul, is the view that humans are reborn to earthly existence after their death. This view has no biblical basis and it has always been rejected by Christianity. In the last couple of decades, however, through New Age thought and the influence of Eastern religions, the belief in reincarnation has increased in the United States.

As early as a thousand years before the birth of Christ, the belief in reincarnation was first present in Hinduism. Variations of it later appeared in Buddhism. In Western culture, the Greek philosophers, some Roman philosophers, the Gnostics, and some of the Greek mystery religions believed in reincarnation. More recently, it was popularized in the occult movement of Theosophy and through psychics such as Edgar Cayce and Jeane Dixon. Reincarnation is also taught in Jainism, Sikhism, Norse mythology, some Native American religions, and Druidism. Scientology also uses an altered concept of the idea.

Christianity and the Bible reject the idea of reincarnation. Hebrews 9:27 is very straightforward: "It is appointed for men to die once and after this comes judgment." We also have the words of Jesus to the thief who was crucified beside Him and believed in Him: "Truly I say to you, today you shall be with Me in Paradise" (Luke 23:43). Jesus offered the thief eternal life and immediate entrance into heaven, not reincarnation.

Douglas Connelly summarizes the human condition, the need for salvation, and the mistake of believing in reincarnation:

> Human beings are not progressing upward to God through an endless cycle of rebirths. Instead we are all lost, dead in our sins and separated from the life of God. What redeems us from that dreadful situation is the grace and forgiveness of God, who, because of the atoning sacrifice of Christ on the cross, is free to forgive those who come to him in faith. . . .
>
> Perhaps reincarnation is becoming more widely accepted in Western culture because it is convenient to believe. It is easier to think that you will return to human life again than that you will have to give an account of this life to God, who has the power to cast people into eternal separation from him. Reincarnation also appeals to human pride by teaching that a person's final destiny rests on human effort, not on the grace or judgment of God. Even human

sin is not looked on as something wrong before God but rather as a learning experience, a potential step in a person's upward progress.[20]

How we live this life and where we will spend eternity are the most important issues that each and every person must decide. This life is not a "dress rehearsal" for another life or for many more lives. You have only one life to live; live it for God.

34. What about near-death experiences?

The subject of life after death has been prevalent in our popular culture for the last couple of decades. Some of the interest has been biblically based, but much of it has not. The majority of the popular literature sold and the discussions on radio and television talk shows has been centered in New Age thought, mysticism, Eastern religions, or the occult.

One of the corollaries of this fascination has been the increase and study of near-death experiences (NDE). NDEs have been widely reported, and many people have claimed an experience categorized as an NDE.[21] Biblical evaluations and evangelical responses to the questions surrounding NDEs are also available and should be read by those who have specific questions about NDE.[22] Gary Habermas and J. P. Moreland provide a helpful distinction on the nature of NDEs:

> We need to make an important distinction between clinical (or reversible) death and biological (or irreversible) death. In clinical death, external life signs such as consciousness, pulse, and breathing are absent. In such cases, biological death virtually always results if no steps are taken to reverse the process. Biological death, on the other hand, is not affected by any amount of attention, for it is physically irreversible. . . . Most near-death reports are from those who were close to clinical death.[23]

When considering an NDE, it is important to remember that the experience is not an after-death experience and therefore cannot provide accurate or legitimate information about the afterlife and heaven. Only the Bible does that. Ron Rhodes writes:

> We must keep in mind that near-death experiences do not actually prove anything about the final state of the dead. After all, these experiences are near-death experiences, not once-for-all completely dead experiences. In fact, as one writer said, near-death experiences "may tell us no more about death than someone who has been near Denver but never within city limits can tell us about that town. Both NDEs (near-Denver and near-death experiences) are bereft of certitude. . . . In both cases, more reliable maps are available."
>
> The map for near-death experiences is, of course, the Bible. Scripture defines death as the separation of the spirit from the body (James 2:26). And true death occurs only once (see Heb. 9:27).[24]

The religious content of an NDE and its significance for the person who experiences it vary widely and are affected by the worldview of the individual. For example, people with New Age religious beliefs report NDEs consistent with that theology and people with other religious beliefs experience NDEs espousing those views. Habermas and Moreland note:

> It makes sense that the identification of the figure [religious figures seen in NDEs] will come from the patient's own background. . . . For instance, no American claimed to have seen Shiva, Rama, or Krishna. . . . It would appear, then, that previous religious, cultural, and sociological beliefs affect the wide differences in NDE interpretations, including the way figures are identified. . . . So there are important reasons that certain factors of interpretation

comment more on a person's beliefs, society, and culture than they do on the facts themselves.[25]

We must also remember that for some people there may be an occultic association with the NDE, and it may be of satanic and demonic origin. Occultic and psychic activities are condemned by God (Deut. 18:10–13), and any participation or involvement with them should be shunned. NDE researcher Jerry Yamamoto gives wise caution regarding NDEs, noting that because they "are of a subjective nature, determining their source is largely a speculative venture. With divine, demonic, and several natural factors all meriting considerations, a single, universal explanation for NDEs becomes quite risky."[26]

Discussion about NDEs is interesting, but it doesn't provide any reliable answers or insights into heaven and eternity, and it has the potential of demonic deception or leading people far from the truth of God's Word. Only the Bible can give us infallible information regarding heaven and life after death. Rhodes provides the following wise counsel on evaluating NDEs:

No matter what kind of experience you have, always test it against Scripture (see 1 Thess. 5:21). If anything contradicts the Word of God in any way, it must be rejected. Make the Scriptures your sole measuring stick. God's Word will keep you on track.[27]

PART 5

What Is the History of Heaven as an Idea?

35. Was there a concept of heaven in the religions of Egypt and the ancient Near East?

The Egyptians were among the first people to have detailed views of the afterlife and were "a race preoccupied with death."[1] It was, however, not a biblical perspective. Egyptian religious views of the afterlife were closely tied to concepts of multiple gods, fertility, abundance, and drew from life as it was experienced in connection to the Nile River and Nile River Valley. It was thought that those who died were taken before Osiris, the god of the dead, and judged, having their heart weighed on scales to see if good deeds or bad deeds prevailed.[2] Closely tied to this was the idea of *ma'at,* a quality that a good person nurtured that involved justice, kindness, order, and being in touch with the fundamental law of the universe. There was also a goddess Ma'at, who was the personification of these virtues and the daughter of the sun god Re (or Ra, of whom the pharaohs were believed to be incarnated sons).[3]

Egyptian ideas of who could enter the presence of the sun god Re changed throughout the centuries. John Casey writes:

In the development of Egyptian beliefs about the afterlife there was a sort of gradual democratization. In the earliest period—the Old Kingdom [2686 B.C.–2181 B.C.]—it was believed that pharaoh and his family alone could ascend to a life of bliss in the heavens, while ordinary people went to the underworld. Later the privilege of joining the god Re in the heavens was extended to members of pharaoh's court and his highest officials. Finally, by the time of the Middle Kingdom [2180 B.C.–1640 B.C.], the "solar" realm of the dead became open to all.[4]

Closely tied to the journey one was thought to make after death were ritual and spells that could be performed by the deceased once they had died and started their journey. Spells recorded in the Egyptian *Book of the Dead,* were written on tomb walls, placed inside coffins, or inscribed on a roll of papyrus that was buried with the mummy.[5]

In Mesopotamia and the ancient Near East, concepts of the afterlife and the location of such existence were closely related to the lives and desires of the gods. Heaven was the realm of the gods, not humans. The Sumerian *Epic of Gilgamesh* tells of the impossibility of immortality, something reserved for the gods. Casey writes:

> The ancient Mesopotamians—the Sumerians, the Akkadians, and the Babylonians—had a view of death infinitely more somber than the Egyptians. There was no happy afterlife in which the whole human being could be restored to full vitality, but only a dark, gloomy, silent netherworld of the dead, who have become mere shades, the "land of no return."[6]

There was no hope of salvation or resurrection. Belief in those things comes only with the biblical record.

36. Was there a concept of heaven in Greek and Roman thought?

Greek and Roman mythologies and religions were very different from Christianity and the teachings of the Bible. Their views of the afterlife were understood to be part of a cycle of birth, life, and death, wherein there was hope for a serene existence after death. But there was no savior or redemption in those religions. In Greek mythology, Elysium, or the Elysian Fields, were the final resting place of departed souls of the heroic and virtuous mortal descendents of Zeus, the god of sky and thunder who ruled from Mount Olympus.

It was believed that most souls did not live in Elysium, but in a bleak place of the underworld known as *hades*. Some heroes of Greek legends were permitted to visit hades. For example, in the myth of Hercules, he is permitted to travel to the underworld to capture the multi-headed hound Cerebus, which guards the gates of Hades (Cerebus is also featured in Roman literature in Virgil's *Aeneid*).

In classical Greek, the word *hades* can refer to either the unseen underworld or the god Hades. In Greek mythology, the god of the underworld was Hades who was the brother of Zeus and Poseidon and who collectively defeated the Titans and claimed rulership over the universe, ruling the underworld, air, and sea, respectively (the solid earth was the domain of Gaia).

Plato believed in the preexistence of the soul and that in this world we do not truly learn, but only remember from the past and that the soul continues after death. In the conclusion of his work *The Republic* (10.614–10.641), there is a story known as "The Myth of Er" that tells the story of a warrior who dies in battle and commences on a journey in the afterlife. The myth was very influential in Greek thought in introducing the idea that moral people were rewarded and immoral people were punished after death. In part it was through this dialogue that Socrates, the main speaker in the work, argued for the judgment of the dead and the immortality of the soul. Aristotle disagreed with Plato's view, arguing that there was no soul after death. What is debated in the study of both Roman and Greek mythology and religion is the degree to which the ideas were accepted in the daily lives of the Greeks and Romans.

Drawing from Greek mythology and building upon it, Roman religion and thought taught the idea that the spirits of the dead were taken across the mythological river Styx to the underworld, where they were judged and sent either to Tartarus (hell) or Elysium (heaven). In the *Aeneid,* Virgil describes Tartarus as a large place surrounded by the flaming river Phlegethon and having triple walls to prevent its inhabitants from escaping.[7] Similar to the hound Cerebus in Greek mythology, Tartarus is guarded by a hydra (serpent or monster) with fifty jaws. Some Romans also believed that the dead, living in tombs, could influence the lives and fortunes of the living. Funerals for Romans were very elaborate events seen as preparation for the journey across the river Styx. Part of this preparation was placing a coin in the mouth or two coins on the closed eyes of the deceased so that they would have money to pay Charon, the ferryman, to transport them across the Styx. (Dante also writes of Charon in *The Divine Comedy,* as does John Milton in *Paradise Lost.*)

37. Was there a concept of heaven in Norse religion?

The oldest sources for information on Norse concepts of heaven and the afterlife appear in thirteenth century works that were compiled from earlier traditions. These works, the *Poetic Edda* and the *Prose Edda,* vary in their descriptions of the afterlife but do attest to Norse belief in it, although it was very different from the biblical perspective. The most commonly mentioned places for the dead in the afterlife were *Valhalla, Helgafjell, Hel,* and *Fólkvangr.*

- *Valhalla* ("Hall of the Slain") was the heavenly abode (similar to the Greek's Elysium) that was reserved for brave warriors who died in battle. It was believed that those who went there were brought to it by valkyries (female figures who decided who would die in battle). Once in Valhalla, the warriors reunite as *einherjar* ("lone warriors") and remained physically fit, preparing as warriors for a final battle of gods and humans at the end of time known as *Ragnarök* ("doom of the gods"). It is this event that German composer Richard Wagner (1813–1883) popularized in the operas *Der Ring des Nibelungen*.

- *Helgafjell* ("holy mountain") was an idea in some Norse sources of a sacred mountain in the afterlife where members of Norse clans lived, leading lives similar to ones they led before death.
- *Hel* ("conceal") was a dreary subterranean realm and the location where those who are evil go after death. It is presided over by a goddess of the same name, the daughter of the god Loki and who was appointed to govern it by Odin, the chief god in Norse mythology.
- *Fólkvangr* ("field of the host") is similar to Valhalla. Half of those who die in combat go to Valhalla and the remainder go to the Fólkvangr. It is ruled over by the goddess Freyja, a goddess associated with love, beauty, fertility, gold, and war. In Scandanavian mythology there was also ancestor worship, based on the belief that if the dead were properly cared for and remembered they would protect the homestead, the family, and the fertility of the land and family.[8]

38. What did the early Christians say about heaven?

Following the teaching of the apostle Paul in 1 Corinthians 15:20–58, early Christians believed in the physical resurrection of the individual body to the place that Jesus Christ is preparing for Christians (John 14:2–3). Much of the thought and importance of the resurrection and heaven for early Christians developed in the context of persecution and martyrdom.[9] Heaven was often depicted for Christian martyrs as a glorified material world free of persecution, pain, and suffering.[10] Also, much of the earliest teaching related more to the resurrection of the body than to the nature of heaven. This early teaching involved the use of metaphors and imagery that drew often on Paul's metaphors of seeds and first fruits, though also with different emphases and nuances.[11]

One of the earliest Christian writings beyond those in the New Testament is the second century work by an unknown author entitled *The Shepherd of Hermas.* It speaks of a world to come in which the righteous will be like living trees that flower.[12]

Early Christians also had to answer pagan critics who derided belief in the resurrection of the body. In response to non-Christian opponents, Theophilus of Antioch (d. 183–85),[13] Justin Martyr (103–165),[14] and Athenagoras of Athens (ca. 133–190)[15] wrote arguments for the resurrection of the body.

The theologian Tertullian (ca. 160–ca. 220) from the Roman province of Carthage was one of the most prolific writers of the early Christians and was an early apologist for Christianity. He strongly affirmed the physical resurrection of the body that would be "liberated by the Lord."[16] Irenaeus joined in this affirmation (ca. 202) in his refutation of heretics *Against Heresies* (*Adversus Haereses*).[17]

Latin theologian and philosopher Augustine of Hippo (354–430) is one of the most influential thinkers of western history. It would be difficult to overestimate the effects of his theology in the West. His work, *The City of God*, is a foundational treatise in theology, political theory, and philosophy. Along with earlier Fathers of Christianity, Augustine affirmed and emphasized the physical resurrection of the human body and believed that heaven is the place where Christians will enjoy God in the fullness of the body and the soul. For Augustine, heaven is the place where human innocence that was lost in the garden of Eden is restored and improved. Humans in perfected resurrected bodies will be conformed not to the image of Adam but to the image of Jesus Christ and will praise God eternally in His presence. It is beyond the capacity of humans to fully understand its nature and glories.[18]

Augustine also taught that each person retains his or her identity since salvation is an individual matter. However, part of the glory and joy of heaven will be the collective worship of all Christians of all ages—the communion of saints in the perfected community that is the body of Christ fulfilling perfectly the Great Commandment of Deuteronomy 6:4–5. The focus of heaven is not the individual, but the worship of God. At the beginning of Augustine's spiritual autobiography he declares, "our heart does not rest until it rests in God."[19] In heaven, that rest will be fully realized as we fully see, love, and worship God forever.[20]

39. What did Christians during the Middle Ages and Renaissance say about heaven?

More than a thousand years passed between the death of Augustine in 430 and the beginnings of the Reformation era in the early 1500s.[21] During these centuries there were many writings on theology coming from monasteries across Europe. It was a vibrant age and not at all the "dark ages" as portrayed by later Enlightenment writers seeking to minimize Christianity.[22] According to McDannell and Lang, "Medieval theologians, artists, poets, and visionaries made the afterlife more visible and accessible—at least to reason and imagination. Heaven became a part of the general world view."[23] Building on cultural concepts, emerging ideas in Western thought, and urban revival (especially after 1150) "three new cultural concepts gave heaven its medieval shape: the city, the intellect, and love."[24]

Whereas earlier theologians had used the imagery of a renewed and perfected garden like the garden of Eden, theologians of the Middle Ages drew from biblical imagery as well as the growth of cities throughout Christendom (increasingly portrayed heaven as the perfect celestial city). Yet, images of heaven as a garden did not disappear, as is evidenced by a widely copied and translated book entitled *Elucidation,* dating from the twelfth century. This book described in detail the new creation and heaven as a fragrant garden.[25] It was also during this time that there was a rise in Christian mysticism, with mystics describing visions of God and redefining relationships with Him.

Many ideas in theology, philosophy, and emerging science (especially astronomy) coalesced as theologians such as Peter Abelard (1079–ca. 1143), Peter Lombard (ca. 1100–1160), and Thomas Aquinas (ca. 1224–1274) sought to systematize theology in what became known as "scholasticism." The rediscovery of the writings of Aristotle also caused theologians to consider the relationship of the universe to heaven. Scholastic theologians accepted Aristotle's cosmology wherein the universe was made of concentric circles and spheres, with the innermost being hell and the outermost spherical shell being the firmament of the universe (an idea also promoted by Dante). Beyond the outermost sphere were two other spheres. The first was the "spiritual heaven," or the "empyrean," that was the abode of the blessed and the angels. Although God presided in the first sphere, it was in the second sphere, the "heaven of heavens," where the Trinity resided. This second sphere was also known as the Heaven of the Trinity and was reserved for God alone.[26] McDannell and Lang write of these two spheres:

> While scholastic theologians refrained from further speculation about the properties of God's abode in the heaven of heavens, they took more interest in the lower abode of the angels and saints, the empyrean. When looked at from the earth, the empyrean appeared as the highest heaven, because it was situated above all the planet-carrying heavenly spheres.[27]

It was the sphere of the empyrean heaven that was thought to be the home of blessed souls following death and that would serve as their eternal abode after the Last Judgment.[28]

The most famous comprehensive and systematic presentation of theology was the *Summa Theologica* of Thomas Aquinas that

was left unfinished at his death. Aquinas followed the thought of
Augustine in much of his work, trying to prove his theology from
Scripture, philosophy, and theological tradition. For Aquinas,
heaven for believers was the empyrean wherein glorified human
bodies would literally shine greater than the sun.[29]

Discussions of and images of light in relation to heaven (with
heaven often represented as pure light) were very prominent in
medieval theology. These ideas of heaven as a place of light were
also literally built in to the cathedrals of the era. Gothic architecture
and cathedral designers—such as the famous cleric Suger (ca. 1081–
1151), Abbot of St. Denis, near Paris—consciously utilized stained-
glass windows for the dual purpose of giving light and teaching
of the brilliance of heaven. McDannell and Lang comment on this
Gothic architecture:

> The concentric circles of light, with light standing for the
> divine and the circle of perfection, were not an invention
> of Dante. . . . By the age of Dante, the huge circular win-
> dows of Gothic cathedrals united the light of divinity and
> the circle of perfection. The large circular "rose window"
> perforated their facades high above the front entrance.
> Whatever other meanings this window received through
> its stained-glass narratives, it also served as a symbol of
> God's presence. While the *Divine Comedy* ends in a vision
> of intangible light, architects and builders made that light
> accessible and tangible.[30]

For the medieval Christian, heaven was literally an integral part
of his or her worldview. Although medieval Christians were wrong
in their astronomy and cosmology, they were applying theology
and the Bible to every area of life and every academic discipline and
vocation. There is much for us to learn, not only in their history and
theology, but also from their spirituality.

As the Renaissance emerged, ideas and images of heaven (and

hell) continued in great detail and were portrayed with diversity and emotion in the arts and science.[31] Renaissance portrayals of heaven were often more sensuous than earlier ones. Art flourished and there were many portrayals of heaven, although not all accurately reflected the biblical text. In art there was also a greater portrayal of individuals in heaven—often friends and family members.

40. What did the Protestant Reformers say about heaven?

One of the themes of the Protestant Reformation was *sola Scriptura*—Scripture alone. The Reformers placed a great emphasis on the biblical text and individual reading and study of the Bible. By the time of the Reformation, the printing press enabled wide distribution of books and ideas giving rise to more information for scholars, clergy, and laity. The Reformation era brought many developments and diverse perspectives in theology. There were central themes common to the Reformers, such as an emphasis on the Bible, the doctrine of grace, salvation by faith alone, and the worship of God.[32]

It was the German Augustinian friar Martin Luther (1483–1546) and French lay theologian John Calvin (1509–1564) who were most instrumental in reforming Western Christianity. Their emphases on the majesty of God and total faith in God for salvation permeated Reformation thought and refocused perspectives on heaven to a highly God-centered perspective.[33] McDannell and Lang observe: "In keeping with their theocentric outlook, the reformers saw eternal life primarily as the individual's unsurpassed communion with God. . . . Luther and [Philipp] Melanchthon's emphasis on the divine as center of both this life and eternal life concurred with the outlook of Calvin."[34] Similarly, McGrath notes: "It was, however, at the time of the Reformation in Western Europe that this theocentric vision of heaven came to dominate Christian thinking. The rise of Calvinism in the sixteenth and seventeenth centuries witnessed the triumph of a God-centered vision of the Christian life, both in the present and future."[35]

Reformation theology taught the importance of life in the present world as well as in the world to come and heaven. Though marred by sin, there was value in nature and the world. McDannell and Lang explain: "Because of their appreciation of the world, the reformers tempered their theocentric heaven and earth with an eternal life that recognized the importance of the earth. Speculation about the distant empyrean heaven of scholasticism, which had no need for a renewed earth, was replaced by a concern for nature and the universe."[36]

Both Calvin and Luther believed in the perfection of plants and animals in the renewed earth that would come in the future after Christ's return. They argued that God would purify the universe such that animals and plants would continue for eternity in their perfected state. However, the new earth was not the home of the redeemed saints—they would reside in heaven. Luther thought the redeemed might occasionally visit the new earth, but Calvin did not think they would have any desire to do so.[37] These ideas show that for the Reformers (and for any person) any thoughts about the theology of heaven are intimately connected with eschatology—the doctrine of future things. A person cannot have a coherent theology of heaven unless he or she thinks about events such as the second coming of Christ, the resurrection of the dead in Christ, future judgments, and the nature of the millennium. All of these things are part of God's plan for the ages.

Luther and Calvin agreed in their belief that individuals would retain their identities and gender in heaven (but not profession or social status). Every person will be equal. All political, ecclesiastical, and social structures (including marriage and the family) will cease to exist. They firmly believed that loved ones would see one another again but households will not be reestablished.[38] Some Reformers, such as Luther and Ulrich Zwingli (1484–1531), stressed the reunion of saints; but others, such as Calvin, downplayed the idea, seeing it as a distraction from the worship of God.[39] Reacting against scholasticism and questions of minutiae regarding heaven,

Calvin encourages readers to resist speculation beyond the limits of Scripture. In a prescient statement he declares: "Let this, then, be our short way out: to be satisfied witht the 'mirror' and its 'dimness' until we see him face to face [1 Cor. 13:12]."[40] In so doing, Calvin demonstrated one of the greatest motivations of the Reformation—the desire to read, study, and know the Bible.

41. How influential were the writings of Dante, John Milton, and John Bunyan on the Christian view of heaven?

The great writings of authors such as Dante, Milton, and Bunyan, who themselves drew upon the images portrayed in the biblical text and graphically communicated them for their readers, have definitely enhanced the imagery of the doctrine of heaven (and hell) for many Christians. Theologian Alister McGrath writes:

> It is arguably the *imagery*, rather than the *theology*, of the New Testament that has had the greatest impact on the development of the notion of heaven in Christian literature. The idea of a heavenly city proved to be a remarkably fertile source of stimulation for Christian writers, seeking to depict a future Christian hope in highly visual and memorable terms.[41]

The literary (and often spiritual) influence of Dante, Milton, and Bunyan has been enormous. Drawing on classical sources—and for Milton, Renaissance sources—as well as theology and the Bible, Dante and Milton provided enduring portraits of heaven and hell. To these John Bunyan added a magnificent story of a person's quest for and journey toward heaven.

Italian poet Dante Alighieri's (1265–1321) masterful 14,000-line epic poem *Divine Comedy* (1308–1321), is considered to be one of the greatest works of world literature. The three-part allegorical vision of the afterlife (*Inferno, Purgatorio, Paradiso*) combines the

medieval worldview and Christian theology, especially the philosophy and theology of Thomas Aquinas.[42] Tracing the imaginary
journey of a soul through purgatory, hell, and heaven, Dante's poem
portrays heaven as pure light, with God as its source and Jesus
Christ at the center surrounded by nine circles of angels. Below the
Trinity and the angels are the redeemed who sit in a rose-shaped
amphitheater contemplating and worshipping God for eternity.[43]

Shortly after the publication of *Divine Comedy,* William Langland's (ca. 1332–ca. 1386) allegorical narrative poem *Piers Plow-
man* spoke of the joys of heaven made possible by Christ throwing
open the gates of death and hell. "Langland's famous dream made
a direct appeal to the deep human longing for something better
than the world known to the senses. . . . The vision of heaven that
so entranced Langland and his many readers proved to have the
power to console those who feel overwhelmed by the sorrow and
pain of this life."[44]

In 1667, John Milton (1608–1674), then blind, published his mas-
terpiece *Paradise Lost.*[45] Milton's heaven "reflected the sparkling
environment portrayed in Revelation and the celestial incandes-
cence of the scholastic heavenly empyrean. . . . Nothing human
marred the perfection of God's home. Heaven, as described by
Milton, was the theocentric heaven of the Puritans."[46] Milton's
heavenly realm of the angels, portrayed in relationship to the garden of Eden before the fall of Adam and Eve, was the model of
perfection for which the undefiled garden of Eden was a distant
shadow and the pleasures of heaven were not unlike those of the
pre-fall garden of Eden.[47] McGrath writes of Milton's portrayal of
the garden of Eden:

> Milton's rich prose draws extensively on classic sources,
> such as Homer's Garden of Alcinous and Hesiod's account
> of the "Isles of the Blessed." Milton here set a trend that
> others would follow. Later works such as Thomas Burnet's
> *Sacred Theory of the World* develop the notion that pagan

fables of paradise were dim and distorted recollections of Eden, thus laying the foundation for the incorporation of the rich classical paradisiacal legacy into the literature of Christianity. Milton's epic transfigures the elements of the biblical account of Eden, as the potent imagery of the Renaissance gardens interplays with its more modest biblical counterpart.[48]

Though Milton writes primarily of the garden of Eden, heaven is always the standard against which Paradise is portrayed.

English literature professor Leland Ryken notes:

> *Paradise Lost* is about heaven—its glory, its reality, its attainability, the obstacles that can keep us from it, and the possibility of bringing its qualities into earthly life. The word "heaven" appears more than four hundred times in the poem. Even though Milton chose epic as his medium, there is a sense in which his goal is the same as that of devotional writers of his day—to convince readers how miserable they are in their state of sin apart from God's salvation, and to delineate how sinners can attain heaven through the life of faith in Christ.[49]

For Milton, the greatest thing about heaven was eternal praise of God, who is the central figure of heaven.

John Bunyan (1628–1688) is one of the best-known Puritan writers, and his book *The Pilgrim's Progress* (1678, 1684) is one of the literary best-sellers of all time.[50] It was read "both as an adventure story—foreshadowing the modern novel—and as an allegory of the struggles, temptations, sufferings, and final salvation of the human soul."[51] The central figure is a person named Christian who flees from the City of Destruction heading for the Celestial City. Bunyan's theology in the book affirms the resurrection of the body and the biblical view of the saved having glorified bodies.

John Bunyan, as much as any other Christian writer, told of the spiritual journey all Christians make in their lives. His pilgrim, Christian, made the same journey and had the same longing that has been shared by Christians throughout the centuries. It was not different from Augustine's of which he wrote in *Confessions* and *City of God*. Nor was it different from those who, in the midst of trials and tribulations, have identified with hymnist Samuel Stennett's lyrics "On Jordan's stormy banks I stand, and cast a wishful eye, to Canaan's fair and happy land, where my possessions lie. I am bound for the promised land."[52]

While John Bunyan's *Pilgrim's Progress* told an imaginary story of a person's spiritual journey, prolific Puritan minister Richard Baxter (1615–1691) offered readers a spiritual guide for daily living that told of the glories awaiting Christians in heaven. His work *The Saints' Everlasting Rest* (1650) emphasized the joys of heaven as Christians lovingly and joyfully worshipped God without distraction.

Many other authors in English literature have written of heaven and its glories, the most prominent being John Donne, George MacDonald, and C. S. Lewis.[53] Heaven has also been a common theme in Christian music through the centuries and was very prominent in African-American spirituals and in English and American hymnody. Literary, musical, and artistic depictions of heaven are abundant in the fine arts.

42. Who was Emanuel Swedenborg and what were his teachings about heaven?

Emanuel Swedenborg (1688–1772) was a Swedish scientist and mystical thinker who claimed direct contact with angels and the spiritual world through dreams and visions as well as in his normal waking hours. He also claimed to have visited all the heavenly realms. He believed that God was commissioning him to create a new religious society (known as the New Church) of all who accepted his doctrines. In 1747 he resigned a position with the Swedish Board of Mines to devote his full energies to his new calling and many writings. He spent the remainder of his life in Sweden, the Netherlands, and London.

Swedenborg's system of thought and writings were based on the idea of a correspondence between the physical world and the spiritual world, wherein the latter consisted of various groupings of deceased individuals that made up a single great human being. He believed that Jesus Christ was the greatest manifestation of humanity, but he rejected the doctrine of Christ's penal substitutionary atonement and salvation through faith alone. He also rejected the biblical and orthodox view of the Trinity. However, his aberrant and heretical Christology, soteriology, and eschatology did find followers and his prolific writing on the spiritual world and heaven found an audience (primarily after his death). Among his writings that deal with heaven are: *Heavenly Secrets* (8 vols., 1749–1756), *The New Jerusalem and Its Heavenly Doctrine* (1758), *Heaven and Hell* (1758), and *The Apocalypse Revealed* (1766).

Swedenborg taught that all angels in heaven were once people on earth and that people of all faiths enter heaven if they followed their religion carefully. He also taught that there is no ultimate end to history on earth and the New Church is the fulfillment of the prophecies of the New Jerusalem in the book of Revelation. McDannell and Lang observe: "Swedenborg's visions of heaven contrasted sharply with the ascetic, theocentric heaven of the Protestant and Catholic reformers. At almost every turn, he offered readers a vigorous alternative to the traditional heaven articulated by medieval theologians and refined by post-Reformation thinkers."[54] Swedenborg's cultural influence was greater than his religious influence but his writings gained popularity in the nineteenth century. His followers today call their movement "The New Church" or "Church of the New Jerusalem." Among the many people influenced by his writings were quite a few thinkers of the day, such as: William Blake (1757–1827) who eventually renounced him, Elizabeth Barrett Browning (1806–1861), Samuel Taylor Coleridge

(1772–1834), Ralph Waldo Emerson (1803–1882), Walt Whitman (1819–1892), Helen Keller (1880–1968), William James (1842–1910), and Robert Frost (1874–1963). Some religious historians also see significant similarities between Swedenborg's views on heaven and those of Joseph Smith, Jr., the founder of Mormonism, and Mary Baker Eddy, the founder of Christian Science.

PART 6

What Do Other Religions Teach About Heaven and Eternity?

43. What does Judaism teach about heaven?

According to Jewish teachings in the Talmud, the universe and created order is comprised of seven heavens: Vilon, Raki'a, Shehaqim, Zebul, Ma'on, Machon, and Araboth. It is the seventh heaven, Araboth, where the throne of the Lord and the angelic seraphim are located. The Jewish mystical literature (Merkavah and Heichalot) as well as literature relating to the biblical figure of Enoch and the apocryphal *Book of Enoch* discusses the details of these heavens. These writings and surrounding traditions eventually became part of the Jewish medieval mystical tradition of Kabbalah.

The spiritual afterlife is referred to in Judaism as Olam Ha-Ba, which is Hebrew for "the world to come" or "afterlife." However, while Judaism includes belief in an afterlife, there is little doctrine and discussion of it in Reform, Conservative, or Orthodox Judaism. When there is discussion, the ideas (as in all faith traditions) are not unanimously accepted and there are a variety of opinions. One rabbi quoted in the Mishnah said that the present life is like a hallway to Olam Ha-Ba, wherein individuals should prepare themselves in this world in the same manner they would if they were in a hallway about to enter a large banquet hall (*Pirkei Avot* 4:21). Rabbinic literature also sometimes uses the term Olam Ha-Ba to refer to the coming messianic era. Additionally, the term is sometimes used interchangeably with the term Gan Eden ("the garden of Eden"), which also is a heavenly realm where souls reside after physical death and suggests a return of the soul to a state similar to the blissful existence of Adam and Eve before their expulsion from the garden of Eden. Many believe then that the "disembodied soul will remain in this state until the time of bodily resurrection in the days of the Messiah."[1]

Some contemporary Jewish sources attribute the relative silence within Judaism regarding death and the afterlife to the fact that the Torah (the Pentateuch or first five books of the Bible) was written very soon after the long Jewish sojourn out of Egypt and because there was a religious and cultural preoccupation with death by the Egyptians. The Egyptian preoccupation is evidenced in part by the important ancient Egyptian funerary text, *The Book of the Dead or Going Forth by Day*, known simply as *The Book of the Dead*, which had its origins in the Old Kingdom era (ca. 2700–2111 B.C.).

However, the lack of details in Judaism about the afterlife, heaven, and hell does not mean that Judaism rejects the concept of the afterlife. Rather, the afterlife is understood as being part of the divine plan wherein evil is overcome by God, who is omnipotent and just. Judaism views attempts to describe the afterlife as speculative, although there is the belief that good people are rewarded.

The resurrection of the dead is one of the 13 Principles of Faith formulated by the great medieval rabbi and philosopher Maimonides (1135–1204) in his commentary on the Mishnah (*Tractate Sanhedrin*, chapter 10): "I believe with perfect faith that there will be a revival of the dead at the time when it shall please the Creator, Blessed be His name, and His name mention shall be exalted for ever and ever."

In Judaism, it is customary for loved ones to recite the mourner's prayer known as the Kaddish ("holy") during the first eleven months after a loved one's death and on the anniversary of the death (*yahrtzeit*) of a loved one. In reciting and praying the Kaddish, the mourner acknowledges the greatness of God. There is no mention of death in the prayer and comfort is found in the idea that the soul of the departed one was regathered by the One Who created it in the first place. The opening words of the prayer are inspired by Ezekiel 38:23, a vision of God becoming great in the eyes of all people and all the nations. The Kaddish is one of the central prayers of Judaism. Although it is sometimes popularly thought of as the Jewish prayer for the dead, that designation is incorrect and more accurately belongs to the prayer known as El Maleh Rahamin ("God full of compassion"). In this prayer, those praying specifically pray for the soul of the deceased asking that it be granted proper rest and complete contentment.

44. What does Islam teach about heaven?

Islamic theology and the teaching of the Qu'ran (which is quoted by Surah, or chapter, of which there are 114) distinguishes between the cosmological heavens of creation arching over the earth and heaven as a place of final rest for the righteous. That latter is normally referred to in Islam as "paradise." Islam also teaches that there are seven heavens as part of the cosmological order (Surah 23:86) and that the distance separating one heaven from another is equal to the distance a person could travel in five hundred years.[2] The seven heavens are: Firdaus (the highest), 'Adn, Na'iim, Na'wa, Darussalaam, Daarul Muaqaaman, and Khuldi (the lowest). It is the lowest heaven that is adorned with the constellations and planets and with meteors that are meant to serve as projectiles against demons (Surah 15:17; 67:5).[3]

In Islamic theology, every person will be resurrected at a future day known variously as "the hour," "reckoning day," "the day of judgment," "the last day," or "the day of resurrection."[4] On that day each individual will be called to face up to his or her good or bad deeds and judged accordingly, and will then dwell in either a state of bliss or a state of damnation for eternity. "Every man shall be pledged for what he earned" (Surah 52:21). The Qu'ran portrays existence in the hereafter as an eternal physical abode in which the inhabitants are living, sensible human beings. While later Islamic works teach eternal punishment of those who do not enter "paradise" (the Islamic name for what Christians call "heaven"), the emphasis of the Qu'ran is on those whose judgment brings reward and entry into paradise. The most common term used for paradise in the Qu'ran is *janna,* which literally means "garden."[5] One author writes of the Qu'ran's concept of eternity stating:

> The Qur'an proclaims God's promise of an eternal reward or punishment for humans in the afterlife as contingent upon their earthly actions. On the day of eternity, the righteous will be told of the pleasures they can enjoy in the garden of eternity with its eternal fruit and shade. They shall live there forever with their spouses. In contrast, those who were evildoers or unbelievers will be put forever in a place of severe chastisement. They are God's enemies since they denied his signs, and God shall forget them in the fire on account of their acts.[6]

Hell is known as al-Nar and Jahannam, and is understood to be a place of eternal fire, with boiling waters, scorching wind, and black smoke (though some interpreters consider these attributes to be metaphorical).

Based upon interpretation of Surah 46:15, many Muslims believe that a person who dies before the age of forty enters the lowest part of heaven—forty is the age of accountability in their thought.[7] About sixty times, the Qu'ran uses the term "righteous deeds" as a guarantee to entry into paradise (cf. Surah 4:122–24) and implicitly restricts paradise to only Muslims (Surah 2:112). Surah 13:20–23 and 70:22–35 mention specific conditions for entering paradise, among them reverence, prayers, charity, and sexual fidelity.[8]

The rewards of paradise are two types: sensual pleasures and spiritual pleasures, of which the greatest is the spiritual reward of dwelling in God's presence. Many interpreters also consider the sensual pleasures to be metaphorical descriptions. The oft-repeated idea that 72 virgins await Islamic martyrs in paradise comes from teachings in a collection of sayings of the prophet Muhammad known as the Hadith (Sunan al-Tirmidhi 2,562), and not from the Qu'ran.

Especially prominent in Islamic tradition is the belief that twelve years after being called as a prophet, Muhammad ascended to heaven, carried there on a winged horse known as a Buraq. This event, the "Night Journey," was comprised of two parts: the Isra and Mi'raj. Muslims believe that it was during the Isra, the first part of the journey, when the archangel Gabriel came to Muhammad bringing the Buraq and then accompanied him to a place known as "the farthest mosque," which is interpreted to be what is now the site of the Al-Aqsa mosque on the Temple Mount in Jerusalem (although there was no mosque there at the time of the Night Journey). On the Temple Mount, known to Muslims as "the Noble Sanctuary," Muhammad is said to have dismounted and tethered the Buraq to the Western Wall (the Wailing Wall) of the remains of the Second Temple while praying.

After prayers, Muhammad began the second part of the journey, the Mi'raj, during which time he was taken to heaven, speaks with Abraham, Moses, and Jesus, and is then taken into the presence of Allah by Gabriel. It was during this time that Allah instructed Muhammad that Muslims were to pray fifty times a day. However at the urging of Moses, Muhammad returns to the presence of Allah, asks for a reduction several times, and is finally given the number five as the daily occurrences of prayer for Muslims. It is from this event that Muslims pray five times daily. It is also from this tradition of the Night Journey that Muslims claim religious significance for the Temple Mount. The Qu'ran records the Night Journey in Surah Al-Israh 17:1 and other details of the tradition come from the Hadith.

45. What does Hinduism teach about heaven?

The worldviews of the religions of the East, such as Hinduism, Buddhism, Sikhism, and Jainism are very different from Christianity. In much of Hinduism, there is a preoccupation with death and what happens in the afterlife. However, there is much inclusiveness and pluralism in Hinduism that makes generalization about Hindu thought difficult. Most Hindu thought holds that the universe has no beginning and no final end, but instead undergoes cycles of creation, dissolution, and recreation. Behind these eternal cycles there is a conscious abstract impersonal principle or divine intelligence known as Brahman, of which individuals play a microcosmic part.[9]

However, a second major view in Hinduism is a theistic view in which there is a Supreme Being, sometimes portrayed as male and sometimes as female, who is responsible for the creation and eventual dissolution of the universe and who is personal and active in the universe and its inhabitants. Common names attributed to this being are Vishnu, Rama, Shiva, and Devi.[10] There are also other gods and goddesses in Hinduism and they often descend from the heavens and are manifested or incarnated and interact with humans. These are known as *avatars*, coming from the Sanskrit word for "descent."

Part of Hindu theology and philosophy is the idea of *moksha*, similar to salvation, that involves the pursuit and achievement of divine knowledge that leads one to self-realization and liberation from the perpetual wheel of *samsara*, the cycle of birth, life, death, and rebirth/reincarnation. According to the wheel of samsara, every action or deed (karma) has a correlating effect on this life and the next, such that good acts have good effects, and bad acts have bad effects. It is a cosmic law in which humans have freewill to act but cannot evade the effects of actions. If one lives a good life, it will be rewarded with a better life and higher consciousness in the next life, and if one lives an evil life, he or she will be reborn as an animal or other unfortunate being in the next life. The cyclical process ends when an individual attains moksha, or release from the cycle of samsara.

Also part of the Hindu view of the afterlife is the concept of the Atman or soul. It is considered one's true self and is eternal and indestructible. Atman may refer to either the universal cosmic self or to the individual soul, also known as *jiva*. It is considered eternal, immutable, and indestructible, and therefore death is only an illusion. Death is ultimately not real.[11]

Religious studies scholar Kenneth Kramer writes about the teachings of the Hindu sacred text *Bhagavad Gita*:

1. The death of one's physical body is inevitable and is not to cause prolonged grief;
2. the subtle dimension of the person (*jiva*) does not die at death, rather takes on a new body;
3. the Eternal Self (Atman) is birthless and deathless, and cannot be destroyed;
4. one who realizes the Eternal Self while yet alive, will not be reborn but, at death, will merge with the Brahman.[12]

When an individual achieves moksha, the soul is believed to be free of the cycle of life and death. This is the goal, and at such a time the soul is, before death, united with the Brahman achieving a condition of pure joy (*ananda*).

According to Hindu cosmology, the universe is divided into three worlds: Svara (heaven or the seven upper regions), Prithiv (earth), and Patala (the seven lower regions or the underworld). In some Hindu writings there is a concept of hell, a place known as Naraka, that is beneath Patala and is a place of torment where sinful souls are taken if they are captured after death. However, neither

Svara or Naraka are considered permanent abodes. (In Buddhism, Naraka is not hell, but a place of purgation for the soul similar to the Roman Catholic idea of purgatory). Svara is not similar to the Christian idea of heaven since it is not eternal and its human inhabitants are thought to be dragged back to earth and rebirth at some point.[13]

46. What does Buddhism teach about heaven?

Historically, Buddhism emerged from Hinduism and it shares Hinduism's cyclical view of history and of individual existence. Both religions share a belief that karma determines each life, assigning to the many lives of a person a series of experiences that can include heavens and hells. However, Buddhism rejects the idea of transmigration of the soul or reincarnation, teaching instead rebirth of a non-eternal soul.

Although the words translated as "heaven" and "hell" are found in many Buddhist scriptures, the meanings are very different from that of Christianity. As noted above, Buddhist ideas of hell are much closer to the Roman Catholic idea of purgatory. Hell in Buddhism is a place where a soul goes to work out bad karma that has accumulated over many lifetimes. It is a temporary place.

Heaven (*svarga*), which is comprised of six realms of the world of senses, is also a temporary place. "These heavens are places where any being can potentially be reborn. Existence in these heavens is essentially the fruit of wholesome or meritorious karma, and is exceedingly pleasant."[14] In the higher of the Buddhist heavens, there is a "complete absence of physical and mental pain."[15] However, a being's presence in these heavens is only temporary and ends once the good karma is exhausted. At that point, rebirth and existence in a lower and less pleasant realm is possible. "Heavenly existence is not entirely free of *duhkha* (suffering) and falls short of the ultimate goal of *nirvana*, which constitutes a complete and final freedom from the sufferings of the round of rebirth."[16]

The ultimate goal of a being is to attain enlightenment and

release from *samsara,* the cycle of rebirth. Once this is achieved, a being achieves nirvana (lit. "blowing out" as in extinguishing the fires of greed, hatred, and delusion). Nirvana is not a place as is heaven in Christianity, but rather is a state of being that can be reached without dying. When a person achieves nirvana and subsequently dies, the death is referred to as *parinirvana* (his or her "fully passing away"), and the last link of life is broken such that the cycle of life, death, and rebirth is broken and the individual will not be born again. What happens after achieving nirvana is unknown and cannot be explained, as it is beyond all conceivable experience. An individual attains nirvana by following the Buddhist path.

47. What does Jainism teach about heaven?

Jainism originated in India around 500 B.C. and is derived from the term *jina* (conqueror). It has many similarities to Hinduism and much Jain teaching and doctrine is concerned with the nature of the soul and its liberation from bondage to the cycle of birth, life, death, and rebirth (*samsara*).

Jains believe that souls are eternal and are neither created nor destroyed. They have perhaps lived millions of existences either as humans or other beings and all beings experience suffering. Because of karma, souls are trapped in samsara. A soul that is trapped in samsara is thought to be suffering even if the individual appears outwardly happy. When a soul becomes fully aware of its nature, it is released from the cycle and also becomes omniscient. The fully aware and omniscient soul liberated from samsara is known as *arhats* or *kevalin.* When the physical body in which that liberated soul exists dies, the liberated soul achieves a state of purity and perfection (*moksha,* also thought of as nirvana) and is then known as *siddha.* "*Siddhas* do not have physical bodies. They reside at the topmost part of the universe, where they exist in a constant state of omniscience and bliss, and have no further dealings with mundane, worldly affairs."[17]

48. What does Zoroastrianism teach about heaven?

Zoroastrianism is a very old religion dating to about 1500 B.C. in Persia. Today it is found primarily in Iran and India. In India, adherents are known as Parsis. The founder was a person named Zarathustra who lived in Persia sometime between 1200 and 600 B.C. Zoroastrian theology is dualistic believing in a good god named Ahura Mazda (also Ohrmazd), and an evil god named Angra Mainyu (also Ahriman). The good god dwells in perfection and light and the evil god dwells in darkness in eternity. There was a cosmic conflict between the two gods and Ohrmazd created the heavens and earth as well as heavenly beings and creatures on earth to assist him in the battle. When Ahriman saw the creation, he tried to destroy it, afflicting it with evil, violence, and suffering.[18]

Zoroastrians believe that the good god will ultimately win, at which time there will be a recreation of the heavens and earth and all that is good. Prior to this event, the dead will briefly enter either heaven or hell before reemerging to pass through a final judgment of a stream of molten metal, after which all will dwell in total perfection with Ohrmazd.[19] After an individual's death there are two judgments to be faced. The first comes right after death, when a person's thoughts and deeds are judged. If good thoughts and deeds outweigh evil ones, the individual's conscience leads him or her across the Bridge of the Separator (Chinvat Bridge) to heaven. If evil thoughts and deeds outweigh good ones, the conscience leads the individual to the bridge from which he or she falls into the abyss of hell. Whether in heaven or hell, the individual then awaits final judgment at the end of time. Heaven and hell are not eternal. "Through judgment, heaven and hell, they are corrected and rewarded, for their part in the great battle between good and evil."[20]

Heaven, known as *garodman* ("abode of song") or *wahisht* ("best place"), is depicted in Zoroastrian holy writings as a physical place. In heaven, righteous souls are thought to enjoy the company of one another, lesser divinities, and the creator god Ohrmazd. Hell, known as *druzman* ("abode of deceit") is also thought to be a physical place paralleling heaven.[21] There is also a place like Limbo, known as *nana* ("different place"), located between earth and heaven "where souls are suspended, each in isolation, experiencing nothing at all—neither joy nor pain, neither warmth nor cold, neither light nor darkness, neither good nor evil."[22]

49. What does Sikhism teach about heaven?

Sikhism arose in the sixteenth century (about the time of the Protestant Reformation) in the Punjab region of what is now India and Pakistan and in the midst of a society divided by Hinduism and Islam. The central teaching of Sikhism is belief in the oneness of God (Ek Onkar). Sikhs believe that there is a highly structured and divine order (*hukam*) to the universe and all that is in it, and every person must submit to it without questioning it. The goal of life is to achieve spiritual liberation (*mukti*—similar to *moksha* in Hinduism) from the cycle of birth, life, death, and rebirth (*awaguan*). Once this liberation from human existence is achieved, the soul is merged with the Supreme Soul (*Parmatma*).

After death, soul (*atma*), which is immortal, either merges with the Supreme Soul or passes from one form of life to another, depending on the karma of the individual in this world. Sikhism very strongly upholds the idea of reincarnation. "Just like one changes clothes, our soul changes life forms."[23] According to Sikhism, when a person dies minions of death (*jam doot*) come and take the soul to a court of judgment where the person's deeds are read to him or her and the individual is then sentenced to a certain amount of time either in a place of pleasure (heaven) or a place of pain (hell) to receive the fruits of the individual's deeds. After a period of time, based upon one's karma, the soul is then reincarnated and sent back into the cycle of births and deaths. Thus heaven and hell are not permanent, but transitory. Once the cycle is broken, the human soul is forever immersed in bliss and unity with the Supreme Soul.[24]

50. What does Baha'i teach about heaven?

The Baha'i faith is a very recent religion founded in 1850 in Iran by a person named Mirza Husayn 'Ali Nuri (1817–1892). He took the name Bahá'u'lláh, meaning "the glory of God." Frequently persecuted in Muslim countries such as Iran, the Baha'i teachings maintain "the purpose of life in this physical world is to show to the greatest extent possible such spiritual qualities as love, justice, patience, compassion, wisdom, purity, and trustworthiness."[25]

Baha'i adherents believe that human beings survive after death as individual spiritual entities (souls) and each soul will "continue to progress in further spiritual worlds towards its ultimate goal of reunion with God."[26] There is, however, only one physical experience for each soul. There is no transmigration or reincarnation.[27] Heaven and hell are not real places in the afterlife, but can occur in this life. "Bahá'i believe that these [heaven and hell] are metaphors for the state of being near to or distant from God. In this sense, one can be in heaven or hell while in this world."[28]

51. What do Chinese religious traditions teach about heaven?

China is an enormous country with a diverse population and long history. When one thinks of religious traditions in Chinese history it is normally Confucianism, Daoism, Buddhism, and popular or folk religion that is considered.[29] The Chinese term for Confucianism is *Ju*. Confucianism is best known as a moral philosophy emphasizing ethical meaning in human relationships. It believes in divine transcendence, an impersonal deity who is the true source of virtue. For humans, true integrity and a life of virtue connects one with cosmic processes of life and creativity so that as this is done, a person forms a trinity with heaven and earth. The Chinese term for "heaven" is ambiguous, shifting from a supreme deity to a moral force and also to the universe. Confucianism seeks to perfect women and men in the present life. Popular Confucianism teaches that every person has two souls, a lower soul (*p'o*) that is buried with the body and becomes a ghost (*guei*), and a second upper soul (*hun*) that becomes a spirit (*shen*) and ascends to the heavenly realms.

Daoism (or Taoism) emphasizes a search for oneness with the *tao,* which is the underlying principle of reality. There is in Daoism a quest for freedom, wherein the aim is to achieve harmony with all that exists through effortlessness, inaction, and meditation. Those who attain this freedom become immortal. Some strands of Daoism are philosophically oriented and others are religiously oriented. For the philosophical Daoist, there is ambivalence or agnosticism about heaven and future life. For the religious Daoist, there is a pantheon of gods, the existence of spirits, and the potential of existing after death in a place like heaven or hell.

In Chinese folk religion, there is an emphasis on ancestor veneration and the spirit world. Gods, ghosts, and ancestors are ever present.

In Chinese history during the Zhou dynasty (1045–241 B.C.), there was a belief in a deity known as *Tian* ("Heaven"), but it was largely an impersonal ambiguous entity. The term eventually became identified with the abode of the gods and ancestors.[30] A phrase often used in Chinese history is *tiamming* (the "mandate of Heaven"), referring to legitimacy granted to a ruling dynasty by heaven based on the family's virtue (*de*). When the virtue diminishes or the dynasty become corrupt, the authority to rule is taken away.[31] Over the centuries, Chinese religions merged and mingled with each other and also spread to other parts of Asia such as Korea and Japan (where Shintoism also thrives), but they also developed unique cultural and religious practices.

PART 7

What Is the Significance of Heaven for Today?

52. Isn't belief in heaven really just escapism?

A firm belief in heaven has been the hope and comfort of Christians through the centuries, but it is not mindless day-dreaming or emotional escapism. In Colossians 3:2, Paul exhorts Christians to "set your mind on the things above, not on the things that are on earth." Yet, because Christians have done just as the Bible commanded, they have been accused of escapism. John MacArthur counters this criticism:

> It may sound paradoxical to say this, but heaven should be at the center of the Christian worldview. The term world-view has gained great popularity over the past hundred years or so. It describes a moral, philosophical, and spiritual framework through which we interpret the world and everything around us. Everyone has a worldview (whether consciously or not).
>
> A proper Christian worldview is uniquely focused heaven-enward. Though some would deride this as "escapism," it is, after all, the very thing Scripture commands: "Set your affection on things above, not on things on the earth" (Col.

3:2 KJV). The apostle Paul penned that command, and his approach to life was anything but escapist.[1]

Throughout the history of Christianity, the criticism by non-Christians and critics that belief in heaven is really just escapism or a psychological crutch to help people deal with this world has persisted. They argue that heaven isn't real; it's just a coping mechanism. But they are wrong; it's a real hope for Christians who know and experience the trials and tribulations of this world.

To believe in heaven does not mean that we ignore this world; it means that we long for a better and eternal world. Joni Eareckson Tada graphically describes this hope:

> I still can hardly believe it. I, with shriveled, bent fingers, atrophied muscles, gnarled knees, and no feeling from the shoulders down, will one day have a new body, light, bright, and clothed in righteousness—powerful and dazzling.
>
> Can you imagine the hope this gives someone spinal-cord injured like me? Or someone who is cerebral palsied, brain-injured, or who has multiple sclerosis? Imagine the hope this gives someone who is manic depressive. No other religion, no other philosophy promises new bodies, hearts, and minds. Only in the Gospel of Christ do hurting people find such incredible hope.[2]

Answering the charge of escapism, Christian philosopher Peter Kreeft writes that the real issue is not escapism, but truth:

> The first and simplest answer to the charge that belief in heaven is escapism is that the first question is not whether it is escapist but whether it is true. We cannot find out whether it is true simply by finding out whether it is escapist. "There is a tunnel under this prison" may be an escapist idea, but it may also be true.

If an idea is true, we want to believe it simply because it is true, whether it is escapist or not. If it is false, we want to reject it simply because it is false, whether it is escapist or not. The only honest reason for anyone ever accepting any idea is its truth.[3]

The truths about heaven are not escapist, but they are inescapable. "Thinking about heaven is not escapism because it determines my essence. . . . Finding my purpose is the exact opposite of escapism; it is finding my essence."[4]

53. What about the sorrow and grief we experience now in this world?

Christians and non-Christians alike suffer hardships, endure pain, lose loved ones, and grieve. But for the Christian there is eternal hope because of the faith placed in the person and work of Jesus Christ. Because of this fact, Paul, who himself endured many hardships and afflictions, was able to say, "For to me, to live is Christ and to die is gain" (Phil. 1:21).

In Psalm 56:8, David says, "You have taken account of my wanderings; put my tears in Your bottle. Are they not in Your book?" God is very aware of our sighs and cries, our tears and fears, and one day He will wipe them all away. For Christians, the grief and sorrow that we experience is real and natural, but it is also temporary. That is one of the reasons why Paul provides the Thessalonians with the encouragement of 1 Thessalonians 4:13–18 and the teaching on the rapture:

But we do not want you to be uninformed, brethren, about those who are asleep, so that you will not grieve as do the rest who have no hope. For if we believe that Jesus died and rose again, even so God will bring with Him those who have fallen asleep in Jesus. For this we say to you by the word of the Lord, that we who are alive and remain until the coming of the Lord, will not precede those who have fallen asleep. For the Lord Himself will descend from heaven with a shout, with the voice of the archangel and with the trumpet of God, and the dead in Christ will rise first. Then we who are alive and remain will be caught up together with them in the clouds to meet the Lord in the air, and so we shall always be with the Lord. Therefore comfort one another with these words.

In Revelation 21:4, John tells us that one day God "will wipe away every tear from their eyes; and there will no longer be any death; there will no longer be any mourning, or crying, or pain; the first things have passed away." What we experience on earth is real, but what we experience in heaven will also be real.

Heaven will be a place where

- there is no more pain,
- there is no more suffering,
- there are no more hardships,
- there are no more tears, and
- there is no more death.

For those who long for heaven, it is like the words in the spiritual, "All my trials, Lord, soon be over." Heaven means healing. Heaven means hope. Heaven means home.

54. Why should I be concerned about heaven?

"Pie in the sky by and by" is the frequent accusation and attitude of those who deny the present application of the truth of heaven. But belief in and knowledge of heaven matters very much and has daily ramifications. We should be concerned about heaven because it pertains to our eternal destiny. For the Christian, it also is an impetus for godly living, evangelism, and daily ministry to others. Joni Eareckson Tada writes of the daily significance of heaven:

> When a Christian realizes his citizenship is in heaven, he begins acting as a responsible citizen of earth. He invests wisely in relationships because he knows they're eternal. His conversations, goals, and motives become pure and honest because he realizes these will have a bearing on everlasting reward. He gives generously of time, money, and talent because he's laying up treasure for eternity. He spreads the good news of Christ because he longs to fill heaven's ranks with his friends and neighbors. All this serves the pilgrim well not only in heaven, but on earth; for it serves everyone around him.[5]

Heaven does matter today. It is a reminder that life will not always continue as it does today (2 Peter 3:2–7). Things will change, and our lives will pass. Sometimes we forget or ignore that fact. We really don't believe it's all going to end, do we? If God hadn't told us differently, we'd all think this parade of life would go on forever. But it will end.

This life is not forever, nor is it the best life that will ever be. The fact is that believers are headed for heaven. It is a reality. And what we do here on earth has a direct bearing on how we live there. Heaven may be as near as next year, or next week; so it makes good sense to spend some time here on earth thinking candid thoughts about that marvelous future reserved for us.[6]

In Romans 8:22–23, Paul writes,

> For we know that the whole creation groans and suffers the pains of childbirth together until now. And not only this, but also we ourselves, having the first fruits of the Spirit, even we ourselves groan within ourselves, waiting eagerly for our adoption as sons, the redemption of our body.

The body of which Paul speaks is the resurrection body that Christians will have in heaven, but the longings are those of this world. John MacArthur expresses this well:

> Although sin has crippled our souls and marred our spirits—though it has scarred our thoughts, wills, and emotions—we who know Christ have already had a taste of what redemption is like. And so we long for that day when we will be completely redeemed. We yearn to reach that place where the seed of perfection that has been planted within us will bloom into fullness and we will be completely redeemed, finally made perfect (Heb. 12:22–23). That is exactly what heaven is all about.[7]

For many questions about heaven, the Bible does not provide either clear answers or any answers. For some concerns, we must rely on theological deduction or consider the silence of Scripture. God has told us what we need to know, not all of what we want to know. Many things we do know, as we have seen in the preceding pages, but there is definitely more silence than we would like. John Ankerberg and John Weldon reflect on this fact:

> But we must also remember that there is far, far more we don't know about heaven than we do know; its beauties and glories are literally inconceivable to us now. We should expect nothing less from a future kingdom prepared by Jesus, Himself, for those He loves and died for (Matt. 25:34; John 14:2). Apart from Christ, there is no such thing as real life—now or forever.[8]

55. How can I be sure I'll go to heaven?

Theologian Carl F. H. Henry said of contemporary society and its citizens, "The intellectual suppression of God in His revelation has precipitated the bankruptcy of a civilization that turned its back on heaven only to make its bed in hell."[9] Is this bold but true statement an accurate reflection of your own spiritual status?

Perhaps you have reached this final question in this booklet and yet do not know for sure what your eternal destiny will be. If so, then this is the most important question of the booklet for you, and we encourage you to consider carefully its contents.

We would like you to know for sure that you have eternal life through Jesus Christ, God's Son. In Revelation, the closing book of the Bible, John issues a last invitation: "The Spirit and the bride say, 'Come.' And let the one who hears say, 'Come.' And let the one who is thirsty come; let the one who wishes take the water of life without cost" (Rev. 22:17). What does this invitation mean?

The image is that of a wedding. The groom has issued an invitation to the bride. The groom is willing, but is the bride willing? In this same way, God has made provision for you—at no expense to you, but at great expense to Him—to enter into a relationship with Him that will give you eternal life. More specifically, the invitation is issued to the one who hears and who is thirsty.

Thirst represents a need: forgiveness of sin. Thus, you must recognize that you are a sinner in the eyes of God: "For all have sinned and fall short of the glory of God" (Rom. 3:23). God is holy and thus cannot ignore anyone's sin. He must judge it. However, God in His mercy has provided a way by which sinful men and women can receive His forgiveness. This forgiveness was provided at a great cost by Jesus Christ when He came to earth two thousand years ago, lived a perfect life, and died on the cross in our place to pay for our sin: "For the wages of sin is death, but the free gift of God is eternal life in Jesus Christ our Lord" (Rom. 6:23). The Bible also says, "Christ died for our sins according to the Scriptures, and that He was buried, and that He was raised on the third day according to the Scriptures" (1 Cor. 15:3–4).

To obtain this salvation and the eternal life that Jesus Christ offers, we must each individually trust that Christ's payment through His death on the cross is the only way that we can receive the forgiveness of our sins, the re-establishment of a relationship with God, and eternal life. "For by grace you have been saved through faith; and that not of yourselves, it is the gift of God; not as a result of works, so that no one may boast" (Eph. 2:8–9). This is why John invites the thirsty to come and enter into a relationship with God through Christ.

Are you thirsty? Do you recognize your sin before God? If you do, then come to Christ. If you do not acknowledge your need for salvation, then you bypass this opportunity. Please don't.

Those who are thirsty and want salvation can express their trust through the following prayer:

> Dear Lord, I know that I have done wrong and fallen short of Your perfect ways. I realize that my sins have separated me from You and that I deserve Your judgment. I believe that You sent Your Son, Jesus Christ, to earth to die on the cross for my sins. I put my trust in Jesus Christ and what He did on the cross as payment for my sins. Please forgive me and give me eternal life. Amen.

If you just prayed this prayer in sincerity, you are now a child of God and have eternal life. Heaven will be your eternal home. Welcome to the family of God! As His child, you will want to develop this wonderful relationship by learning more about God through study of the Bible. You will want to find a church that teaches God's Word, encourages fellowship with other believers, and promotes the spreading of God's message of forgiveness to others.

If you were a Christian before reading this booklet, we encourage you to continue in your relationship with Christ. As you grow, you will want to live for Him in light of His coming. You will want to continue to spread the message of forgiveness that you have experienced. As you see God setting the stage for the end-time drama of events, you should be motivated to increased service until He comes. May your heart be occupied with His words:

Behold, I am coming quickly, and My reward is with Me, to render to every man according to what he has done. I am the Alpha and the Omega, the first and the last, the beginning and the end." Blessed are those who wash their robes, so that they may have the right to the tree of life, and may enter by the gates into the city. (Rev. 22:12–14)

Conclusion

We live and die in a fast-moving world. C. S. Lewis once remarked about spiritual matters and our frequent preoccupation with worldly concerns that "all that is not eternal is eternally out of date."[1] Everywhere we turn, people, including ourselves, are busy. But are we busy doing the right things? Or are we so focused on the present—and, at times, the past—that we miss or neglect the future? Gary Habermas and J. P. Moreland have written of heaven:

> The God of the universe invites us to view life and death from His eternal vantage point. And if we do, we will see how readily it can revolutionize our lives: daily anxieties, emotional hurts, tragedies, our responses and responsibilities to others, possessions, wealth, and even physical pain and death. All of this and much more can be informed and influenced by the truths of heaven. The repeated witness of the New Testament is that believers should view all problems, indeed, their entire existence, from what we call the "top-down" perspective: God and His kingdom first, followed by various aspects of our earthly existence.[2]

Heaven is indeed a unique and wonderful place, a location that far exceeds our imagination and comprehension. For the Christian, it is a present hope and eternal home. "Heaven is a realm of inexpressible glory."[3] The decision you make about heaven and the free offer of salvation based on the death of Jesus Christ is the most important decision you will ever make. Take care of your soul; you will have it for eternity.

Notes

Introduction

1. C. S. Lewis, *Mere Christianity* (New York: Simon and Schuster, 1996), 119 (Book III, Ch. 10).
2. Steven J. Lawson, *Heaven Help Us!* (Colorado Springs: NavPress, 1995), 16.

Part 1: What Is Heaven?

1. For examples from classical literature, see Wilbur M. Smith, *The Biblical Doctrine of Heaven* (Chicago: Moody Publishers, 1968), 28–29.
2. John F. MacArthur, *The Glory of Heaven* (Wheaton, IL: Crossway, 1996), 56.
3. Ibid., 59–60.
4. Ibid., 60.
5. Gary R. Habermas and J. P. Moreland, *Immortality: The Other Side of Death* (Nashville: Thomas Nelson, 1992), 150.
6. For a graphic portrayal and description of prophecy yet to be fulfilled, including the New Jerusalem, see Tim LaHaye and Thomas Ice, *Charting the End Times: A Visual Guide to Understanding Prophecy* (Eugene, OR: Harvest House, 2001).
7. J. Dwight Pentecost, *Things to Come: A Study in Biblical Eschatology* (Grand Rapids: Zondervan, 1958), 580.

8. Arnold G. Fruchtenbaum, *Footsteps of the Messiah: A Study of the Sequence of Prophetic Events* (Tustin, CA: Ariel Ministries, 1982), 366.

9. For a further discussion of Jerusalem in prophecy by the authors, see *The Truth About Jerusalem in Bible Prophecy* (Eugene, OR: Harvest House, 1996). See also, Randall Price, *Jerusalem in Prophecy: God's Stage for the Final Drama* (Eugene, OR: Harvest House, 1998).

10. John F. Walvoord, *Major Bible Prophecies: 37 Crucial Prophecies That Affect You Today* (Grand Rapids: Zondervan, 1991), 404. For a larger study of the millennium, see Walvoord's *The Millennial Kingdom* (Grand Rapids: Zondervan, 1959).

11. Charles C. Ryrie, *Basic Theology* (Wheaton, IL: Victor Books, 1986), 515.

12. The chart is from Ryrie, *Basic Theology*, 516. Used by permission.

Part 2: What Will Heaven Be Like?

1. See Wilbur M. Smith, *The Biblical Doctrine of Heaven* (Chicago: Moody Publishers, 1968), 190–200; Don Baker, *Heaven: A Glimpse of Your Future Home* (Portland, OR: Multnomah, 1983); and Douglas Connelly, *After Life: What the Bible Really Says* (Downers Grove, IL: InterVarsity, 1995), 101–103.

2. Smith, *Biblical Doctrine of Heaven,* 190.

3. Baker, *Heaven,* n.p.

4. Steven J. Lawson, *Heaven Help Us!* (Colorado Springs: NavPress, 1995), 52–66.

5. Baker, *Heaven,* n.p.

6. Ibid.

7. Joni Eareckson Tada, *Heaven: Your Real Home* (Grand Rapids: Zondervan, 1995), 39.

8. John F. MacArthur, *The Glory of Heaven* (Wheaton, IL: Crossway, 1996), 133.

9. Randy Alcorn, *Heaven* (Wheaton, IL: Tyndale, 2004), 253-61.

10. Alister E. McGrath, *A Brief History of Heaven* (Oxford: Blackwell Publishing, 2003), 37–38. See also, Alcorn, *Heaven*, 288–91.

11. On the subject of Christians and cremation, see David W. Jones, "To Bury or Burn? Toward an Ethic of Cremation," *Journal of the Evangelical Theological Society* 53:2 (June 2010), 335–47.

12. MacArthur, *Glory of Heaven,* 139.

13. Daniel R. Lockwood, "Until We Meet Again," *Christianity Today* (October 2007), 98.

14. Alcorn, *Heaven,* 335, 336. See also, 346–51 on concerns for loved ones not in heaven and other relationships.

15. MacArthur, *Glory of Heaven*, 136.

16. Alcorn, *Heaven,* 373.

17. Gary Habermas and J. P. Moreland, *Beyond Death: Exploring the Evidence for Immortality* (Wheaton, IL: Crossway Publications, 1998), 106.

18. See for example, J. Frewen Moor, *Thoughts Regarding the Future State of Animals.* London: Simpkin & Co., 1899; G. H. Pember, *Animals: Their Past and Future,* reprint ed. Louisville: Cross Reference Imprints, 2002; and Stephen H. Webb, *On God and Dogs: A Christian Theology of Compassion for Animals.* New York: Oxford University Press, 1998. See also C. S. Lewis, *The Problem of Pain.* New York: Macmillan, 1962.

19. For an excellent and recent detailed discussion of animals and heaven, see Alcorn, *Heaven,* 373–90. See also, Roman Catholic philosopher Peter Kreeft's *Everything You Ever Wanted to Know About Heaven* (San Francisco: Ignatius Press, 1990), 45–46. See also, C. S. Lewis, *The Problem of Pain* (New York: Macmillan, 1962), 139–43. For a view that does not hold to animals in heaven, see John Gilmore, *Probing Heaven: Key Questions on the Hereafter* (Grand Rapids: Baker, 1989), 130–33.

20. On the biblical doctrine of angels, see C. Fred Dickason, *Angels Elect & Evil*. Rev. ed. (Chicago, Moody Publishers, 1995).

21. Charles C. Ryrie, *Basic Theology* (Wheaton, IL: Victor Books, 1986), 121–22.

22. Alcorn, *Heaven*, 275–76.

Part 3: Who Will Be in Heaven?

1. John F. MacArthur, *The Glory of Heaven* (Wheaton, Ill.: Crossway, 1996), 129.

2. Daniel R. Lockwood, "Until We Meet Again," *Christianity Today* (October 2007), 98.

3. This material is summarized from Gary R. Habermas and J. P. Moreland, *Immortality: The Other Side of Death* (Nashville: Thomas Nelson, 1992), 114.

4. Ken Gire, *Instructive Moments with the Savior* (Grand Rapids: Zondervan, 1992), 75.

5. Ron Rhodes, *The Undiscovered Country* (Eugene, OR: Harvest House, 1996), 102. See also, Randy Alcorn, *Heaven* (Wheaton, IL: Tyndale, 2004), 340–42.

6. Rhodes, *Undiscovered Country*, 101.

7. Ibid., 101–102.

8. Ibid., 107.

9. Ibid., 108, 205n.12.

10. Robert Lightner, *Heaven for Those Who Can't Believe* (Schaumburg, IL: Regular Baptist Press, 1977), 22.

11. Steven J. Lawson, *Heaven Help Us!* (Colorado Springs: NavPress, 1995), 81.

12. MacArthur, *Glory of Heaven*, 142.

Part 4: What Does the Future Hold for Non-Christians?

1. For a complete study of the issue, see Ramesh P. Richard, *The Population of Heaven* (Chicago: Moody Publishers, 1994).

2. Quoted in John Ankerberg and John Weldon, *The Facts on Life After Death* (Eugene, OR: Harvest House, 1992), 41.

3. C. S. Lewis, *The Great Divorce* (New York: Macmillan, 1946), 69.

4. Gary R. Habermas and J. P. Moreland, *Immortality: The Other Side of Death* (Nashville: Thomas Nelson, 1992), 159.

5. Ibid.

6. The best historical overview of the development of the idea of purgatory is Jacques Le Goff, *The Birth of Purgatory,* Trans. Arthur Goldhammer (Chicago: University of Chicago Press, 1984). See also John Casey, *After Lives: A Guide to Heaven, Hell, & Purgatory* (New York: Oxford University Press, 2009).

7. *Compendium of the Catechism of the Catholic Church* (2005), Q. 210, http://www.vatican.va/archive/compendium_ccc/docu ments/archive_2005_compendium-ccc_en.html#I%20 Believe%20in%20the%20Holy%20Spirit, accessed July 2, 2010. For more about purgatory, see also, R. J. Bastian, "Purgatory," in *New Catholic Encyclopedia,* 2nd ed. (Washington, D.C.: The Catholic University of America, 2003), 11:824–29.

8. *Catechism of the Catholic Church,* Section 1030, http://www.vatican.va/archive/catechism/p123a12.htm accessed July 2, 2010.

9. Ibid., Section 1032.

10. Jacques Le Goff, *The Birth of Purgatory* (Chicago: University of Chicago Press, 1984), 334.

11. Diarmaid MacCulloch, *The Reformation: A History* (New York: Penguin, 2004), 580–81. See Luther's *Small Catechism,* Q. 211 and Calvin's *Institutes of the Christian Religion,* Book 3.5.7–10.

12. Bastian, "Purgatory," *New Catholic Encyclopedia,* 11:825.

13. P. J. Hill and K. Stasiak, "Limbo," in *New Catholic Encyclopedia,* 8:591.

14. Ibid.

15. Habermas and Moreland, *Immortality,* 169.

16. Ibid., 169–76. See also William Crockett, *Four Views on Hell* (Grand Rapids: Zondervan, 1992), for a "pro and con" treatment of all of the major views regarding hell; and Robert A. Peterson, "Does the Bible Teach Annihilationism?" *Bibliotheca Sacra* 156 (Jan.–March 1999): 13–27.

17. Ron Rhodes, *The Undiscovered Country* (Eugene, OR: Harvest House, 1996), 121–23.

18. Charles C. Ryrie, *Basic Theology* (Wheaton, IL: Victor Books, 1986), 521.

19. Rhodes, *Undiscovered Country,* 122–23.

20. Douglas Connelly, *After Life: What the Bible Really Says* (Downers Grove, IL: InterVarsity, 1995), 44–45.

21. Ankerberg and Weldon, *Facts on Life After Death,* 9. See also Habermas and Moreland, *Immortality,* 87; and Rhodes, *Undiscovered Country,* 149.

22. See especially Habermas and Moreland, *Immortality,* 73–105; Rhodes, *Undiscovered Country,* 149–67; Ankerberg and Weldon, *Facts on Life After Death;* and John Ankerberg and John Weldon, *The Facts on Near-Death Experiences* (Eugene, OR: Harvest House, 1996). For a biblical critique of Betty J. Eadie's popular but unbiblical *Embraced by the Light* (Thorndike, MA: G. K. Hall, 1993) see Doug Groothius, *Deceived by the Light* (Eugene, OR: Harvest House, 1995).

23. Habermas and Moreland, *Immortality,* 73.

24. Rhodes, *Undiscovered Country,* 164.

25. Habermas and Moreland, *Immortality,* 91–92.

26. Jerry Yamamoto, "The Near-Death Experience," *Christian Research Journal* (Spring 1992): 5.

27. Rhodes, *Undiscovered Country,* 167.

Part 5: What Is the History of Heaven as an Idea?

1. John Casey, *After Lives: A Guide to Heaven, Hell, & Purgatory* (New York: Oxford University Press, 2009), 23. See also Jeffrey A. Spencer, *Death in Ancient Egypt* (New York: Penguin, 1982).

2. Casey, *After Lives*, 23–25.

3. Ibid., 25.

4. Ibid., 31.

5. Ibid., 30.

6. Ibid., 44.

7. Virgil, *Aeneid*, lines 539–52.

8. For a fuller description of Norse beliefs see John Lindow, *Norse Mythology: A Guide to Gods, Heroes, Rituals, and Beliefs* (New York: Oxford University Press, 2002). See also, Tony Allan, *Vikings: The Battle at the End of Time* (London: Duncan Baird, 2010).

9. See Caroline Walker Bynum, *The Resurrection of the Body in Western Christianity, 200–1336* (New York: Columbia University Press, 1995), 21–53.

10. Colleen McDannell and Bernhard Lang, *Heaven: A History* (New Haven: Yale University Press, 1988), 48–53.

11. Bynum, *Resurrection of the Body*, 24–27.

12. *Shepherd of Hermas*, 53.

13. Theophilus of Antioch, *Theophilus to Autolycus*, 1.13.

14. Justin Martyr, *Fragments of the Lost Work of Justin on the Resurrection*, trans. M. Dods, ed. Alexander Roberts and James Donaldson (Edinburgh: T&T Clark, 1867).

15. Athenagoras the Athenian, *The Treatise of Athenagoras the Athenian, Philosopher and Christian, on the Resurrection of the Dead*.

16. Tertullian, *De resurrectione carnis*, 32 and 57.

17. Iranaeus, *Against Heresies*, 5.31.

18. Jeffrey Burton Russell, "Heaven, Paradise," in *Augustine Through the Ages: An Encyclopedia*, ed. Allan D. Fitzgerald (Grand Rapids: Eerdmans, 1999), 420. See also, McDannell and Lang, *Heaven*, 59–66.

19. Augustine, *Confessions*, 1.1.

20. Augustine, *The City of God*, 22.30.

21. For an overview of the history of thought about heaven

during these centuries, including ideas of heaven in Eastern Orthodoxy and Celtic Christianity, see Jeffrey Burton Russell, *A History of Heaven: The Singing Silence* (Princeton, NJ: Princeton University Press, 1997), 77–113.

22. See Rodney Stark, *The Victory of Reason* (New York: Random House, 2006) and Peter Brown, *The Rise of Western Christendom*. 2nd ed. (Oxford: Blackwell, 2003).

23. McDannell and Lang, *Heaven,* 69.

24. Ibid., 69–70.

25. Ibid., 70–72.

26. Ibid., 82. See also McGrath, *A Brief History of Heaven*, 54–58; and Russell, *History of Heaven,* 120–22.

27. McDannell and Lang, *Heaven,* 82.

28. Ibid., 83.

29. Ibid.

30. Ibid., 85.

31. Ibid., 111–44.

32. For an overview of the era, see Alister E. McGrath, *Reformation Thought: An Introduction*. 3rd ed. (London: Wiley-Blackwell, 2001).

33. McDannell and Lang, *Heaven,* 147.

34. Ibid., 148.

35. McGrath, *A Brief History of Heaven,* 143.

36. McDannell and Lang, *Heaven,* 153.

37. Ibid., 154.

38. Ibid., 154–55.

39. Ibid., 115; 375n19.

40. John Calvin, *Institutes of the Christian Religion,* Bk. III.25.12 (McNeill edition, vol. 2, p. 1007).

41. McGrath, *A Brief History of Heaven,* 17.

42. For an overview of Dante's work, see Casey, *After Lives,* 281–92; Russell, *A History of Heaven*; and Barbara Reynolds, "Dante's Vision of Heaven," in *Journey to the Celestial City,* ed. Wayne Martindale (Chicago, Moody Publishers, 1995), 45–56.

43. McDannell and Lang, *Heaven,* 84–88.

44. McGrath, *A Brief History of Heaven,* 138.

45. For an overview of Milton's work, see McDannell and Lang, *Heaven,* 231–333; Leland Ryken, "Finding Heaven in Milton's *Paradise Lost,*" in *Journey to the Celestial City,* ed. Martindale, 57–77; John R. Knott, Jr. "Milton's Heaven," *PMLA* 85:3 (May 1970), 487–95; and C. S. Lewis, *A Preface to "Paradise Lost"* (New York: Oxford University Press, 1942).

46. McDannell and Lang, *Heaven,* 230.

47. Ibid., 230–31.

48. McGrath, *A Brief History of Heaven,* 70.

49. Ryken, "Finding Heaven in Milton's *Paradise Lost,*" 76.

50. For an overview of Bunyan's work, see E. Beatrice Batson, "In This World and the Next: Bunyan's *The Pilgrim's Progress,*" in *Journey to the Celestial City,* ed. Martindale, 79–87.

51. McGrath, *A Brief History of Heaven,* 29–30.

52. Samuel Stennett, "On Jordan's Stormy Banks I Stand," 1787.

53. For an excellent overview of Christianity in English literature, see Paul Cavill and Heather Ward, et al, *Christian Tradition in English Literature: Poetry, Plays, and Shorter Prose* (Grand Rapids: Zondervan, 2007).

54. McDannell and Lang, *Heaven,* 183.

Part 6: What Do Other Religions Teach About Heaven and Eternity?

1. Rabbi Or N. Rose, "Heaven and Hell in Jewish Tradition," http://www.myjewishlearning.com/beliefs/Theology/Afterlife_and_Messiah/Life_After_Death/Heaven_and_Hell.shtml (accessed June 26, 2010).

2. Tirmidhi, *Sunnan,* no. 3220.

3. Maher Jarrar, "Heaven and Sky," in Jane Dammen McAuliffe, ed. *Encyclopedia of the Qur'an,* (Leiden: Brill, 2002), 2:411.

4. Leah Kinberg, "Paradise," in McAuliffe, ed. *Encyclopedia of the Qur'an,* 4:12.

5. Ibid., 12–13.
6. Shahzad Bashir, "Eternity," in McAuliffe, ed. *Encyclopedia of the Qur'an*, 2:54.
7. An Authorized English Version of the Qu'ran, trans. Dr. Rashad Khalifa, http://submission.org/suras/app32.html (accessed on June 30, 2010).
8. Kinberg, "Paradise," in *Encyclopedia of the Qur'an*, 4:17.
9. Anne Mackenzie Pearson, "Hinduism," in *How Different Religions View Death and Afterlife*, ed. Christopher Jay Johnson and Marsha G. McGee, 2nd ed. (Philadelphia: The Charles Press, 1998), 111.
10. Ibid., 112.
11. *Bhagavad Gita*, 2.19–22.
12. Kenneth Kramer, *The Sacred Art of Dying* (Mahwah, New Jersey: Paulist Press, 1988), 33.
13. Pearson, "Hinduism," 122.
14. Rupert Gethin, "Heavens," in *Encyclopedia of Buddhism*, ed. Robert E. Buswell Jr. (New York: Macmillan, 2005), 1:315.
15. Ibid.
16. Ibid.
17. Emma Salter, "Jainism, Beliefs," in *Introduction to World Religions*, gen. ed. Christopher Partridge (Minneapolis: Fortress Press, 2005), 173.
18. John Hinnells, "Zoroastrianism, Beliefs," in *Introduction to World Religions*, ed. Partridge, 247–48.
19. Ibid., 248.
20. Ibid., 249.
21. Jamsheed K. Choksy, "Zoroastrianism," in *How Different Religions View Death and Afterlife*, ed. Johnson and McGee, 258.
22. Ibid., 258–59.
23. "Sikh Beliefs—What happens after death?" http://www.realsikh ism.com (accessed July 6, 2010).
24. "Q. This idea of reincarnation is rejected from the 3 major reli-

gions. Once again was Hinduism right?" http://www.whyichose sikhism.com/?p=answers&ans=9 (accessed July 6, 2010).

25. Moojan Momen, "The Bahá'í Faith, Beliefs," in *Introduction to World Religions*, ed. Partridge, 424.

26. Ibid., 425.

27. John S. Hatcher, "Baha'i Faith," in *How Different Religions View Death and Afterlife,* ed. Johnson and McGee, 20.

28. Ibid.

29. For an overview of Chinese religions, see Joseph A. Adler, *Chinese Religious Traditions* (Upper Saddle River, NJ: Prentice Hall, 2002).

30. Ibid., 26–27.

31. Ibid. 27.

Part 7: What Is the Significance of Heaven for Today?

1. John F. MacArthur, *The Glory of Heaven* (Wheaton, IL: Crossway, 1996), 50.

2. Joni Eareckson Tada, *Heaven: Your Real Home* (Grand Rapids: Zondervan, 1995), 53.

3. Peter Kreeft, *Heaven: The Heart's Deepest Longing* (San Francisco: Ignatius Press, 1989), 164.

4. Ibid., 170.

5. Tada, *Heaven,* 110.

6. Ibid, 15.

7. MacArthur, *Glory of Heaven,* 123.

8. John Ankerberg and John Weldon, *The Facts on Near-Death Experiences* (Eugene, OR: Harvest House, 1996), 40.

9. Carl F. H. Henry, *Twilight of a Great Civilization* (Westchester, IL: Crossway, 1988), 143.

Conclusion

1. C. S. Lewis, *The Four Loves* (New York: Harcourt Brace Jovanovich, 1960), 188 (Ch. VI).

2. Gary R. Habermas and J. P. Moreland, *Immortality: The Other Side of Death* (Nashville: Thomas Nelson, 1992), 186.

3. John F. MacArthur, *The Glory of Heaven* (Wheaton, IL: Crossway, 1996), 81.

Recommended Reading

The authors are not in agreement with all of the information contained in the books listed below, but they are valuable works on the subject and are a beginning point for further study of the multifaceted topic of heaven.

Adler, Joseph A. *Chinese Religious Traditions.* Upper Saddle River, NJ: Prentice Hall, 2002.

Alcorn, Randy. *Heaven.* Carol Stream, IL: Tyndale House, 2004.

Allan, Tony. *Vikings: The Battle at the End of Time.* London: Duncan Baird, 2010.

Ankerberg, John, and John Weldon. *The Facts on Angels.* Eugene, OR: Harvest House, 1995.

_____. *The Facts on Life After Death.* Eugene, OR: Harvest House, 1992.

_____. *The Facts on Near-Death Experiences.* Eugene, OR: Harvest House, 1996.

Baker, Don. *Heaven: A Glimpse of Your Future Home.* Portland, OR: Multnomah, 1983.

Benware, Paul N. *Understanding End Times Prophecy: A Comprehensive Approach.* Chicago: Moody Publishers, 1995.

Brown, Peter. *The Rise of Western Christendom.* 2nd ed. Oxford: Blackwell, 2003.

Bynum, Caroline Walker. *The Resurrection of the Body in Western Christianity, 200-1336.* New York: Columbia University Press, 1995.

Casey, John. *After Lives: A Guide to Heaven, Hell, & Purgatory.* Oxford: Oxford University Press, 2009.

Cavill, Paul, Heather Ward, Matthew Baynham, Andrew Swinford, John Flood, and Roger Pooley. *Christian Tradition in English Literature: Poetry, Plays, and Shorter Prose.* Grand Rapids: Zondervan, 2007.

Connelly, Douglas. *After Life: What the Bible Really Says.* Downers Grove, IL: InterVarsity, 1995.

Crockett, William. *Four Views on Hell.* Grand Rapids: Zondervan, 1992.

Dickason, C. Fred. *Angels Elect & Evil.* Rev. ed. Chicago, Moody Publishers, 1995.

Fitzgerald, Allan D., ed. *Augustine through the Ages: An Encyclopedia.* Grand Rapids: Eerdmans, 1999.

Fruchtenbaum, Arnold G. *Footsteps of the Messiah: A Study of the Sequence of Prophetic Events.* Tustin, CA: Ariel Ministries, 1982.

Gilmore, John. *Probing Heaven: Key Questions on the Hereafter.* Grand Rapids: Baker, 1989.

Gire, Ken. *Instructive Moments with the Savior.* Grand Rapids: Zondervan, 1992.

Groothius, Doug. *Deceived by the Light.* Eugene, OR: Harvest House, 1995.

Habermas, Gary, and J. P. Moreland. *Beyond Death: Exploring the Evidence for Immortality.* Wheaton, IL: Crossway, 1998.

_____. *Immortality: The Other Side of Death.* Nashville: Thomas Nelson, 1992.

House, H. Wayne. *Charts of World Religions.* Grand Rapids: Zondervan, 2006.

Ice, Thomas and Timothy J. Demy. *The Truth About Jerusalem in Bible Prophecy.* Eugene, OR: Harvest House, 1996.

Jeffrey, Grant R. *Heaven: The Last Frontier.* Toronto: Frontier Research, 1990.

Johnson, Christopher Jay and Marsha G. McGee, ed. *How Different Religions View Death and Afterlife.* 2nd ed. Philadelphia: The Charles Press, 1998.

Jones, David W. "To Bury or Burn? Toward an Ethic of Cremation." *Journal of the Evangelical Theological Society* 53:2 (June 2010): 335–47.

Knott, John R., Jr. "Milton's Heaven," *PMLA* 85:3 (May 1970): 487–95.

Kramer, Kenneth. *The Sacred Art of Dying: How World Religions Understand Death.* New York: Paulist Press, 1998.

Kreeft, Peter. *Everything You Ever Wanted to Know About Heaven.* San Francisco: Ignatius Press, 1990.

_____. *Heaven: The Heart's Deepest Longing.* San Francisco: Ignatius Press, 1989.

LaHaye, Tim and Thomas Ice. *Charting the End Times: A Visual Guide to Understanding Prophecy.* Eugene, OR: Harvest House, 2001.

Lawson, Steven J. *Heaven Help Us!* Colorado Springs: NavPress, 1995.

Le Goff, Jacques. *The Birth of Purgatory.* Trans. Arthur Goldhammer. Chicago: University of Chicago Press, 1984.

Lewis, C. S. *A Preface to "Paradise Lost."* New York: Oxford University Press, 1942.

_____. *The Four Loves.* New York: Harcourt Brace Jovanovich, 1960.

_____. *The Great Divorce.* New York: Macmillan, 1946.

_____. *Mere Christianity.* New York: Simon and Schuster, 1996.

_____. *The Problem of Pain.* New York: Macmillan, 1962.

Lightner, Robert. *Heaven for Those Who Can't Believe.* Schaumburg, IL: Regular Baptist Press, 1977.

Lindow, John. *Norse Mythology: A Guide to Gods, Heroes, Rituals, and Beliefs.* New York: Oxford University Press, 2002.

Lockwood, Daniel R. "Until We Meet Again," *Christianity Today* (October 2007), 98.

MacArthur, John F. *The Glory of Heaven.* Wheaton, IL: Crossway, 1996.

MacCulloch, Diarmaid. *The Reformation: A History.* New York: Penguin, 2004.

Martindale, Wayne, ed. *Journey to the Celestial City.* Chicago: Moody Publishers, 1995.

McDannell, Colleen and Bernhard Lang. *Heaven: A History.* New Haven: Yale University Press, 1988.

McGrath, Alister E. *A Brief History of Heaven.* Oxford: Blackwell, 2003.

_____. *Reformation Thought: An Introduction.* 3rd ed. London: Wiley-Blackwell, 2001.

Moor, J. Frewen. *Thoughts Regarding the Future State of Animals.* London: Simpkin & Co., 1899.

Partridge, Christopher, ed. *Introduction to World Religions.* Minneapolis: Fortress Press, 2005.

Pember, G. H. *Animals: Their Past and Future,* reprint ed. Louisville: Cross Reference Imprints, 2002.

Pentecost, J. Dwight. *Things to Come: A Study in Biblical Eschatology.* Grand Rapids: Zondervan, 1958.

Peterson, Robert A. "Does the Bible Teach Annihilationism?" *Bibliotheca Sacra* 156: 621 (Jan.–March 1999): 13–27.

Price, Randall. *Jerusalem in Prophecy: God's Stage for the Final Drama.* Eugene, OR: Harvest House, 1998.

Rhodes, Ron. *Angels Among Us.* Eugene, OR: Harvest House, 1994.

_____. *The Undiscovered Country.* Eugene, OR: Harvest House, 1996.

Richard, Ramesh P. *The Population of Heaven.* Chicago: Moody Publishers, 1984.

Russell, Jeffrey Burton. *A History of Heaven: The Singing Silence.* Princeton, NJ: Princeton University Press, 1997.

Ryrie, Charles C. *Basic Theology.* Wheaton, IL: Victor Books, 1986.

Smith, Wilbur M. *The Biblical Doctrine of Heaven.* Chicago: Moody
    Publishers, 1968.

Spencer, Jeffrey A. *Death in Ancient Egypt.* New York: Penguin,
    1982.

Stark, Rodney. *The Victory of Reason.* New York: Random House,
    2006.

Stowell, Joseph M. *Eternity.* Chicago: Moody Publishers, 1995.

Tada, Joni Eareckson. *Heaven: Your Real Home.* Grand Rapids:
    Zondervan, 1995.

Walvoord, John F. *Major Bible Prophecies: 37 Crucial Prophecies
    That Affect You Today.* Grand Rapids: Zondervan, 1991.

_____. *The Millennial Kingdom.* Grand Rapids: Zondervan, 1959.

Webb, Stephen H. *On God and Dogs: A Christian Theology of
    Compassion for Animals.* New York: Oxford University
    Press, 1998.

About the Authors

Timothy J. Demy has authored and edited more than two dozen books on the Bible, theology, and current issues. He has also contributed to numerous journals, Bible handbooks, study Bibles, and theological encyclopedias. A professor of military ethics at the US Naval War College, he served more than twenty-seven years as a military chaplain in a variety of assignments afloat and ashore with the US Navy, US Marine Corps, and US Coast Guard. He has published and spoken nationally and internationally on issues of war and peace and the role of religion in international relations. He also serves as an adjunct professor of systematic theology at Baptist Bible Seminary.

In addition to his theological training, which he received at Dallas Theological Seminary (ThM, ThD), Dr. Demy received the MSt in international relations from the University of Cambridge and MA and PhD degrees from Salve Regina University, where he wrote about C. S. Lewis. He also earned graduate degrees in European history and in national security and strategic studies and was the President's Honor Graduate from the US Naval War College.

He is a member of numerous professional organizations, including the Evangelical Theological Society, the Society of Biblical Literature, and is Fellow of the Royal Society of Arts (UK). He and his wife, Lyn, have been married thirty-two years.

Thomas Ice is Executive Director of the Pre-Trib Research Center in Lynchburg, Virginia, which he founded in 1994 with Dr. Tim LaHaye to research, teach, and defend the pretribulational rapture and related Bible prophecy doctrines. He is also an Associate Professor of Systematic Theology at Liberty University and Seminary. Ice has authored and coauthored more than thirty books, written hundreds of articles, and contributed to several study Bibles and theological encyclopedias. He is a frequent national and international conference speaker on topics in prophecy and theology. He served as a pastor for fifteen years prior to his present ministry. Dr. Ice has a BA from Howard Payne University, a ThM from Dallas Theological Seminary, and a PhD from Tyndale Theological Seminary; he is also a PhD candidate at the University of Wales. He is a member of several professional organizations including the Evangelical Theological Society. He lives with his wife, Janice, in Lynchburg, Virginia, and they have three grown sons.